Vivi Duarte

WHO SHE THINK SHE IS?

Your Guide to Developing an Action Plan
and Making it Happen

Foreword by
Aline Midlej
anchor at *Globo News*, and writer for *Vogue Brasil*

WeBook Publishing - English Edition

Published by WeBook Publishing – Los Angeles, CA
All rights in the English language reserved.

This book is a work of nonfiction. It is based on the author's professional and personal experiences while navigating the corporate and entrepreneurial worlds. The opinions and methods described within this book are the author's personal findings. You may discover there are other methods and materials to accomplish the same end result.

For information, please email info@webookpublishing.com

First English Edition
Paperback

ISBN: 978-1-966892-11-3
LCCN: 2025901109
Written by Viviane Duarte
Translator: Nathalia Coppa
Foreword by: Aline Midlej
Editor: Ana Silvani
Copy Editor: Maria Acero
Cover Design: WeBook Publishing
Interior Formatting: WeBook Publishing

Manufactured in the United States of America

Note: Much care and technique were employed in editing this book. However, there can be no assurance that it will be free of minor typing errors, printing issues, or even conceptual ambivalence. In any such case, we ask that the issue be notified to our customer service at info@webookpublishing.com. Thank you!

I dedicate this book to the women who came before me,
my ancestors, who endured everything so I could be where
I am now.

To my granddaughter, Luiza, who awakens my courage to fight for
a society that honors girls and women.

Get up and go to a mirror.

Do you see who you are?

Now is the time to sign an agreement with

who you are

and who you desire to be.

Map out your plans:

Plan 1: Face life's bullshit

Plan 2: Make allies

Plan 3: Start with what you have.
Even if that's nothing.

Plan 4: Put faith and value in yourself

Plan 5: Learn to negotiate

Plan 6: You first!

Plan 7: Show yourself to the world

Plan 8: Be the leader of your plans

Plan 9: Align dreams to purposes

Plan 10: Leave a legacy

Table of Contents

Foreword

Aline Midlej, Brazilian Journalist, anchor at *Globo News*,
and writer for *Vogue Brasil*.

No matter who we are, we dream.

"Luck favors those who work for it." That's just one of the many truths you'll find in this book, each backed by lived experiences. Without ignoring the historical weight of gender, race, and class, Viviane Duarte delivers a practical and deeply human guide to prosperity for girls and women. Drawing on years of experience across boardrooms and the undeserved outskirts of Brazil, she gives voice to strategies forged in both struggle and resilience.

Changing your life might start with a radical new habit: stop complaining, reframe the sabotaging thoughts, and build a better relationship with your mind. We all dream, at least, we should.

When I was invited to write the foreword for *Who She Think She Is?* I instantly felt the power of this book would extend beyond Brazil to women around the world who still navigate what it means to succeed without shame, judgment, or self-sabotage. Despite cultural differences, the weight of stigma and prejudice touches us all. That is why sharing these stories across borders is so essential.

To speak of Viviane Duarte, our beloved "Vivi" as we call her here in Brazil, is an honor. She's an extraordinary entrepreneur, but never conventional. She builds to include, never relying on clichés or performative activism. Vivi created her own method for overcoming adversity, one rooted in courage and accountability. Her NGO, *Plano de Menina* (A Girl's Plan), is like a lighthouse and a world of possibilities. It doesn't just empower girls from underserved communities to dream; it transforms everyone who encounters her work, including me.

With high-quality training and real-world connections, Vivi has already transformed the lives of hundreds of individuals. That, dear readers, is a legacy in motion. It's sisterhood in its most honest and transformative form, a living example that when one woman rises, she lifts others with her. And it works.

What Vivi dreamed for herself, she now dreams for all women, especially Black and poor women, because she was once one of them. Vivi dreams in bold, vibrant colors. She rolls up her sleeves and builds bridges where there once were walls. The very title of this book is a provocative invitation to reflect, a gentle but firm nudge in a world filled with external noise and too little internal listening to hear our true essence.

Reading Vivi's story feels like reconnecting with a long-lost friend. There's a warmth and wisdom in her words that hold you tight and lovingly push you forward. She reminds us that while life doesn't come with a map, we carry inner compasses that, when we learn to trust them, make the journey not easier, but more conscious, more powerful, and yes, more joyful.

The image of young Vivi, with plastic bags wrapped around her feet to protect her from the heat and mud of São Paulo's outskirts, embodies a poetic force that transcends the raw reality. In that determined girl lived the seeds of a future strategist, a born negotiator who learned survival from her mother and grandmother, two women who turned scarcity into ingenuity and everyday life into an art form. That kind of wisdom doesn't come from textbooks.

This isn't a fairytale. As the author herself makes clear, this book doesn't sugarcoat reality. It speaks honestly of pain, victories, tears, and triumphs. Holding her baby in one arm and a college degree in the other, Vivi chose not the easy path, but the meaningful one. She founded *Plano Feminino*, a creative agency with a mission to rewrite the narrative, challenging sexism and reclaiming how women are portrayed in media.

Who She Think She Is? goes far beyond biography. It's a roadmap for personal and professional growth, packed with tools, truths, and a healthy dose of laughter. Vivi's voice blends lived experience with refreshing clarity, offering practical tools that read like emotional first aid for women ready to rise.

As I turned the pages, I felt I was in a heartfelt conversation with a wiser friend, one unafraid to show her scars because she knows that scars tell stories worth sharing. Vivi's courage invites us to face our struggles head-on, to build networks that support us, and to believe that we deserve to dream big and take up space.

In a world that still tries to box us in, label us, or tell us who we can and cannot be, this book is a rallying cry. *Who She Think She Is?* asks us to step out of the line of conformity, take hold of the pen, and write our own stories with boldness and intention.

So, prepare to be challenged and moved. But most of all, to be called into action. Vivi Duarte's words are healing and fuel. Let this book be your guide to a life with greater meaning, joy, and audacity. Because as she reminds us: the road might be tough, but with focus, faith, and a little humor, we'll get there. She did it. And she never arrives alone. Let's go? Because no matter who we are, we dream. And we all deserve to.

To the Anonymous Entrepreneurs, with Love.

Every morning, Jane wakes up to prepare fresh delicacies for her clients. Many Janes, Marys, Annes, and Sarahs are transiting through the streets with large bags. Many know them as street vendors, but others would call them peddlers. However, what they are is warriors. Survivors.

These women may not even know what the word 'entrepreneurship' means. Perhaps they believe this toil is just a part of life, and they are simply doing what they need to do to pay the rent, cover their children's classes, and put food on the table. They can't even imagine the strength they carry in their bags.

These women give meaning to the word "entrepreneur." Most of them, far away from spotlights, university classrooms, and MBA programs, are transforming their lives and those around them. They are tireless. They don't want to increase the scalability of their business, much less create a franchise model and expand. They want to be exactly where they are. They want to pay the bills doing what they believe they do best.

These women have emptied themselves to fill themselves with faith, courage, and purpose. And no, the goal was never, and probably never will be, to leave their communities. Instead, they try to provide happiness and a bit more comfort to their loved ones. With their businesses, they are changing out the furniture in their homes, clothing the children, and covering for the weekend barbecues. Their bills are always paid on time. Their name is their most considerable heritage, and they honor their word. They're superwomen. Stunning. Inspiring.

When you come across one of these women on the street:

Stop. Admire. Observe. Learn.

You will see they have a sparkle in their eyes and an amount of hope that makes us suffocate. You'll notice that all the energy they have will make you question what you've done with all you have. So, you'll sigh. And maybe renew your hope that so much can be done with so little. While you head home thinking about this and going to sleep with the image of these women in your mind, they'll be preparing for the next day. To wake up at the crack of dawn with smiles on their faces. Anonymous. Fulfilled.

Who She Think She Is?
Vivi Duarte

CHAPTER 1

Have A Plan For Everything

Who She Think She Is?

Vivi Duarte

The week I turned 41, I decided I would write my book. I've been writing it in my head for almost a year, and I realized that everything would escape in the first week of my 41st year. I don't know how to explain how I arrived at this conclusion. Better yet, perhaps I do know: intuition. Do you listen to yours?

After many years of overthinking it, I learned to listen to my intuition. I've gotten myself into so many situations by not listening to those butterflies in my stomach screaming, "Go for it!!!" or my liver yelling, "Stoooop!"

Do you know when it feels like you're making it all up in your head, or is there a silly little fear in the back of your mind? A while ago, I decided to listen to that. Our bodies tell us everything, and we just need to be open to listening to it. Turn on those antennas, love!

When you have a plan and move through the world shouting it from the rooftops, showing that you're not messing around, you attract everything, even the bad things.

When you have a dream, you don't necessarily have the obligation to remain silent and keep it secret. But it is essential to pay attention to your body, its sensations, and intuitions in the face of circumstances and people who appear before your journey.

Everything in life is about choices. Knowing how to choose your allies and those you'll listen to is also good. Spoiler:

only you know what you're capable of accomplishing. We'll talk about this more in this book.

The other day, I went to a spa to get a massage and rest my body. I was exhausted from carrying *The Woman* (the universal image of the woman each of us wants to be), so I decided to be on my back for a while. It looks heavy, right? And it is! Being born a woman without privileges, living in a society without access to quality education and opportunities, and being able to get where I am while preserving my mental health is rare. Very rare. How many women, and girls like me, were left behind? Thousands.

Just look at the research results conducted by the American NGO Save the Children. According to them, among 144 nations evaluated worldwide, Brazil ranked 102 on the Girls' Opportunity Index. Across the American continent, Brazil is only ahead of Guatemala and Honduras. This index considers data on child marriage, adolescent pregnancy, maternal mortality, representation of women in government, and completion of secondary education. "Brazil is one of the most unequal countries in the world and with fewer opportunities for women and girls who are born in lower-income areas, especially black women," the study concludes.

I often say that I feel like I'm twice my age. I don't mean my disposition—despite the masseuse at the spa saying that my sciatica is inflamed from so much stress and that I should book a pack of massages for more relaxation (Help!). I'm referring to my experiences and the obstacles I've overcome to carry out my plans and achieve my goals. To gain access to spaces like this spa and receive that massage. Do you know how?

Stories like mine often appear in the media as fairytales with spectacular headlines like: "She made it!" These articles are always accompanied by a perverse meritocratic narrative that refuses to look at inequalities and to understand that stories of women who are born without social privileges and achieve their goals are the exception, not the rule.

For example, seeing your parents being evicted from their home because they don't have money to pay the rent. Much less seeing your mother leave early for work and return late at night with no time to talk to you. She had no time for herself. All of this, it's nothing like a fairytale.

I don't think it's a heroic princess story for you to live on an unpaved street in a dangerous neighborhood or have to use plastic bags on your feet when going up or down the street because when it's hot, it's like a Sahara Desert with almost three feet of soft soil. And when it rains, the street looks like a sea of slippery mud.

Where's the poetry in that?

I could tell you a story starting at chapters of my life where I was already outside this social context, but do you know why I prefer to start from the beginning? Because I respect my story and that of millions of women like me, my mother, and my grandmother who live in Brazil. Women who seek to make their dreams come true but are faced with a lack of social privilege, sexism, domestic violence, lack of self-esteem, and faith in themselves caused by exhaustion.

Maybe you were born into a better social condition than me and, even so, have your thorns along the way. We all do. Regardless of the circumstances into which we were born, all of us are underestimated and conditioned to establish shallow plans and have little ambition simply because we're women.

We are trained to serve.
Despite being in the 21st century,
we must be beautiful, modest,
and domestic.
We are conditioned to be perfect
in a society that demands from
us wonderful breasts, the hair
from a shampoo commercial,
and the sculptural body of a TV
protagonist.
We are influenced daily to use
filters on social media, love
Photoshop, and follow
imprisoning beauty standards.

Vivi Duarte

As I wrote this book, *Globo TV* was airing a soap opera called *A Dona do Pedaço*. The protagonist was Juliana Paes (a famous Brazilian actress), with her toned body, tanned skin, and a wide smile. She played a character that I identified with right from the start. A girl who grew up learning her grandmother's recipes and eventually started selling cakes to survive. Since soap operas like to show us fairytales just like social media, it only took the character a few episodes to become a wealthy businesswoman by selling her cakes.

So I ask myself: How long will they tell us stories of perfect female warriors and make us believe that to bring your plan to life and to become a successful woman, you need to have a waist like Juliana Paes and believe in a scenario as perfect as the one on TV? Where are the slaps in the face we receive behind the scenes? The installments of tax payments? The pile of bills? And what about the anxiety that gnaws at our creativity?

We are constantly bombarded by stories that only leave us anxious. In them, achievements happen quickly. Women are perfect. The problem always comes with an instant solution. You feel tension and even guilt for not achieving the same results as the women the media typically presents to us, be it in soap operas or magazines. But there is one question you need to ask yourself before comparing: Where did that person start from?

You need to respect your story and understand that each of us starts at a different reality and that it's not good to compare yourself to another woman or person. Never compare yourself! You, your story, and your plans are unique. Take everything you've acquired during these years of life, and I'm not just talking about money but your support network, contacts, and good and bad experiences. This has an intangible and precious value that no money can buy. These are your assets. Your tools to win.

Gather everything, including the dreams of the girl you once were. What would you say to her today? Have plans been lost? Did you change the route? Have you cowered in the face of adulthood and hid behind badges and roles in a company? Were you frozen in time because of a relationship? Have you progressed and overcome a lot? Bring together every lesson and moment you've experienced so far, love. All of this has value. Believe it!

WRITE TO YOURSELF

What would you say to the girl you once were?

Do you remember the dreams you had before adulthood and how your responsibilities disconnected you from such childhood ambitions?

Who is The Woman you thought you wanted to be?

Write a letter to yourself and celebrate all the accomplishments you've had up until now.

FROM ME TO ME:

_____

_____

_____

_____

_____

_____

_____

_____

_____

_____

_____

_____

_____

_____

_____

_____

_____

_____

_____

_____

_____

_____

CHAPTER 2

Clichés That Save Plans

"LOOK AT LIFE AS A GLASS HALF FULL…"

Do yourself a favor and stop complaining about everything. I did this, and so much changed. It's difficult, but you can do it. Whenever you have a pessimistic view of things and situations, pause, take a deep breath, and retrace the steps of your thoughts. Teach your mind to work for you.

Neuroscience discusses this extensively, and research has proven that pessimism can be self-sabotaging. Stop!

"THE EARLY BIRD GETS THE WORM"

No one is asking you to wake up with the chickens. Everyone has their biological clock and daily schedule. However, it is a trap to think that everything that is yours is set aside, and you won't need to go after it to carry out your plans. Luck comes to those who work hard and chase what they want. The rest become the audience.

Get up and go after it!

"TELL ME WHO YOU WALK WITH AND I'LL TELL YOU WHO YOU ARE"

Who are your allies? Who is in your network of support? Who have you had coffee with in the past month? Build a network of people who have the same purpose as you. Networking is more than a game of being interested in another person. It's a game of mutual interests in which one person contributes to the other and creates bonds of trust. Invest in sincere relationships beyond roles and company badges. Interesting and interested people are very different from selfish people—remember that for life.

"IF YOU WANT SOMETHING DONE RIGHT, DO IT YOURSELF"

If it's your plan, there's no point in outsourcing the execution. You must pay attention to every detail and roll up your sleeves. Delegate, yes. Outsource plans, never! Outsourcing is the path to failure.

My mother, Shirlei, and grandmother, Nica, said phrases like these almost daily. And I often rolled my eyes (as a tired teenager does). But they were right and knew what they were talking about all along. They usually found solutions where none existed. I realize this by looking at the circumstances of our house during my childhood. We lived in a tenement and had no money to do anything extraordinary. But my mother and grandmother didn't see the situation that way and always carried out their plans with what they had available. Everything always had a solution at home, even if that meant selling your lunch to pay for dinner. We always had a plan.

In this book, I will share with you all the lessons I've learned by seeing setbacks become opportunities, as well as everything I've been learning throughout my twenty-year career. It's been ten years as an entrepreneur, partner, proprietor, and CEO of my life, from bill exterminator to conqueror of powerful plans.

I will tell you everything so that you stay alert and join the game of the business world, whether as an entrepreneur or in any other role you aspire to. I will introduce you to tools you can use to hack the classist, sexist, and patriarchal system that exists in our society. My goal is for you to occupy the best spaces and become the protagonist of your own story. And of course, always remember: one goes up and pulls the other, agreed?

TERM OF COMMITMENT WITH MYSELF

I, _____, commit to putting
myself first in every situation in my life, understanding that this
is not selfishness but self-love and self-prioritization.

I promise to let go of toxic people around me who don't believe
in my plans and always put me down.

According to this term, I declare myself the owner and sole
proprietor of my plans and guardian of myself, only maintaining
the things that add value by my side.

If there's no added value, goodbye!

Starting now, my plan is *(write your plan here)*:

Signed _____

Date _____

Who She Think She Is?
Vivi Duarte

CHAPTER 3

Face Life's Bullshit

Who She Think She Is?

Vivi Duarte

Ever since I was 6 years old, I have wanted to be a journalist. I lived in a tenement in São Paulo with my mother, sister, and father. Mrs. Antônia and my friend, Alice, lived in the same backyard. There was also Tadeu and his grandmother, who always shouted: "Tadeu, where are youuuu?" His aunts would remove his lice in the sun with a fine-toothed comb and crush the bugs under their nails. Ick!

On the street where I lived, there were beautiful houses (ours was the simplest), and the children in these homes had certain privileges. Some families had their own cars and houses, and their children attended English and ballet classes while studying in private schools.

These children ate sliced bread with mayonnaise every day. I thought that was incredible. In my house, we only had sliced bread on birthdays. My mother would prepare a sardine and mayonnaise paste to spread on the bread and cut it into delicious squares to serve to my friends.

At that time, I didn't know that was a class privilege nor that my family was poor. In fact, my mother never told me. I think she did that because, in her mind, being poor was a matter of state of mind.

My mother and grandmother were always entrepreneurs but never mentioned that word. They would say that they "sold their lunch to pay for the dinner," and that everything was okay because, at the end of the day, there was always food on the table. We lived happily. My father was a vendor and sold stuffed animals and raffle tickets on the street. It was a race to survive and overcome life's obstacles on the outskirts.

I grew up accompanying my grandmother to one of the most popular vendor neighborhoods in São Paulo, *Brás*. People from all over Brazil go there to buy and resell various products. She purchased and negotiated with local traders in such a charming way that filled me with pride. She always got what she wanted and fought for it. We'd returned home with bags full of sweets and clothes to resell. I always got the candy that came with a ring. I collected and loved them even if they'd get dark quickly.

That was our life. Our way of staying on our feet amidst the difficulties.

Even with so much difficulty, my mother and grandmother had a thing in common that differentiated them from other women living in that tenement. They had plans. And these plans weren't small. They both dreamed of seeing my sister and me enter college—me in the journalism program, and my sister in business. We were raised for that: to not give up in the face of challenges or lower our heads to problems or deprivations.

My mother always taught me to face life's bullshit from an early age. A girl once laughed at my outfit because I was wearing pants we recycled from one of my uncles. I arrived home devastated, and my mother lifted my head and said:

Who She Think She Is?

Vivi Duarte

"What is most important right now for you to achieve your dreams? Name brand jeans or your computer class?" I replied that I didn't know, and she soon helped me understand. "Let's think about it...You'll use the name-brand pants for a year or two, and they will get run down. During that time, what will they teach you? What will they leave you with, and what will you be able to use to become a smarter girl, capable of making her dreams come true?"

I wanted to respond by saying that the pants would make me beautiful, wonderful, and more powerful, but deep down, I knew what she was talking about. With an embarrassed voice, I simply replied, "Nothing..."

My mother wasn't one to flatter us. She was firm, and I believe that if she had let her guard down, I might not have made it to this moment, writing this for you. She lifted my head again, looked me in the eyes, and firmly said, "So, lift your head and go study. Focus on your books and your classes. Pants don't make anyone's dreams come true, my daughter."

Of course, I wanted the new pants. I didn't like using revamped pants and facing the judging looks the girls at my school gave me. I knew my mother was right. Every day, I decided that my dream was bigger than anything else, including the name-brand pants.

WHAT'S YOUR VERSION OF "REVAMPED PANTS?"

Is there something you would've liked to own or achieve, but often, you prioritize something completely different that stops you from fulfilling your dreams? What has made you sabotage your plans? It can be an object, a belief, or any other reason that may paralyze and distract you from what matters. Don't fall for this trap!

You must have consumption awareness and financial education to carry out your plans. Aim for your goal and move firmly towards it. Don't live based on appearances. Having a plan implies commitment and discipline to accomplish it. Otherwise, you will be part of a group of people who continually start and never finish anything—the kind that gets lost along the way.

To carry out your plans, ensure your objectives are clear and well-defined while managing your budget. Before making a purchase, ask yourself: Do I really need this? Will this help me reach my goals, or will it hinder me? Try to maintain your financial life to get your plans off paper. Stay alert because misguided investments can push everything down the drain.

CUSTOMIZE AND CREATE YOUR IDENTITY

In the end, you know what I learned from the revamped pants? I learned how to embroider, tear, shred, and create. I started adding my own style to them. Surprisingly, the girls at school asked me to help them do the same with their designer pants. That's what it's all about: love. It's about valuing and making things happen with what you have in your hands.

THERE WAS A HOLE IN THE MIDDLE OF THE PATH

At a certain point in my life, my family and I moved to a place very far from what we were used to. We left the neighborhood, *Freguesia do Ó*, and went to a metropolitan city in São Paulo called *Franco da Rocha*. We lived on a hill very far from the city center. It was quite challenging to get there as the streets were not paved and had many holes. Our most used accessory at that time was the plastic bags from the supermarket.

Tutorial for dribbling dust and mud

When it was very sunny and the weather was dry, the mud on the street turned into fine, fluffy dust, and because of that, our feet sank and raised dust with every step taken. When it rained, everything became mud, and we'd get stuck at every step. We had to improvise, and the plastic bags were an indispensable accessory for those who needed to get to work or school, minimally safe from all that. We'd put our feet in plastic bags and tie them around our ankles. With this, our shoes and clothes became less dirty. Occasionally, I'd slip and get all my clothes dirty and have to go back home to change.

Until then, we had never lived on an unpaved street. Even in tenements and cohabits, my mother always found a way to find well-located and safe housing. But the family's financial situation was worse than expected, and that was the only possible address for us at the time.

I saw my mother undertaking and working to exhaustion, and my part was to study and help her sell the things she made or resold.

I found the clientele with my *sales expertise* and identified them by conducting a socioeconomic profile analysis, specifically through the garages of their homes. If they had a car, I assumed they had the purchasing power to buy our cakes, plastic food storage containers, and everything else my mother had in stock. Most of the time, my analysis was accurate, and I managed to sell a lot. I saw an opportunity in chaos and didn't stop halfway to question the plastic bags on my feet. We equipped ourselves with whatever we could to maintain our focus on *The Woman* I dreamed of being. And fought for her every day!

You can do this for yourself now. Honor *The Woman* you are and the one you want to become. Take your eyes off the chaos and focus on yourself and your dreams. Build a tutorial for yourself to face the difficulties of your day-to-day life. Be it streets of mud, dust, annoying people, whatever it may be. Put together your tutorial now and honor *The Woman* you are and the one you want to create!

MY TUTORIAL FOR FACING DAY-TO-DAY CHALLENGES

List below five actions that you can start doing today to honor The Woman you are and focus on achieving your goals:

1.

2.

3.

4.

5.

CHAPTER 4

THE DAY I SOLD A SHRUB AND LEARNED A LESSON

Who She Think She Is?
Vivi Duarte

I was born into a family of saleswomen, vendors, and survivalist entrepreneurs. Women who had no choice but to use creativity and all their energy to support their families. Their commerce and clients have always been their greatest allies.

All the hardships of my childhood and adolescence taught me to face life's bullshit head-on without batting an eye. Climbing hills of soft soil and mud taught me how to physically and emotionally balance myself amid the storms that arose and that still arise today. I learned to be resilient.

I often felt like giving up and not attending school or my computer class. That muddy hill and hour-long walk was too hard to face with a backpack full of books and plans too ambitious for a girl like me. However, my focus on becoming who I wanted to be was more significant than the hill and all the other obstacles I faced. I knew I needed to move, or nothing would happen. I'd end up stuck on that hill, isolated from my dreams and the whole world. Public policies, international NGOs, and social projects wouldn't reach me there.

In my mind, giving up wasn't an option. I knew I couldn't sabotage myself. Draw a parallel between your low self-esteem days and the toxic people around you. Think about how many times you've self-sabotaged.

Self-sabotage is the enemy of following through with your plans. Strengthening your self-esteem is the best weapon to silence the little voice that whispers in your ear, saying you'll never achieve your dreams. You can and you will! Tell that little voice to get out of there. Now!

Have you ever let go of a dream because you felt incapable? Either because you heard the voice of a pessimistic person or your own, discouraging you from being The Woman you dreamed of?

Many of my friends gave up. They listened to people who'd say college was not for the poor. These same friends would listen to their toxic boyfriends who would claim to go clubbing alone if they were to spend their time studying.

Many looked in the mirror and invalidated themselves, thinking they were stupid, as their teachers had said, and that they would never amount to anything in life because they had no skills. That wasn't true. We all have skills, and we just need to invest in our self-esteem to find them.

For a girl without privileges to pursue her goals in Brazil, she has to fight five times harder and take countless factors into consideration. I would've certainly had many friends graduating with degrees if low self-esteem and self-sabotage hadn't had such a significant influence.

Have you ever given up on something because you didn't believe you were capable? Felt exhausted from the invalidation of people who should believe in you? Have you discredited your own potential? This feeling is highly present in the lives of us women, particularly if we are experiencing a moment of success. Have you ever felt like you weren't qualified to occupy a position or unprepared to take on new and greater paths? Or have you ever met a woman who experiences this feeling? This lack of faith in yourself did not come out of nowhere. This is a reflection of a patriarchal and sexist system that, regardless of where we came from, tries to convince us we weren't born to accomplish our goals or become protagonists in our own stories.

This feeling has a name: Imposter Syndrome. It's something that's been debated by many scholars.

Those who suffer from this syndrome feel like a fraud and believe their achievements are due to luck and not their abilities, values, and skills.

Research conducted by the Dominican University of California pointed out that imposter syndrome affects around 70% of successful professionals, especially women and students of postgraduate and master's degrees.

Growing up, I always believed in myself. But, as soon as I entered the corporate world and occupied other spaces, I felt incapable. I was afraid to share my ideas and be ridiculed. People talked about their international experiences, and I was silent. All I had to talk about were the floods I encountered while getting to work and the overcrowded trains I took with men leaning on me. What's interesting about that? I felt that at any moment, HR would call me in and tell me that hiring me had been a mistake. What a nightmare!

Maybe you feel like an imposter or incapable of getting your plan off paper. Perhaps you've opened many doors only for people to criticize you without ever having done a third of what you do. You might be feeling tired and have started to believe that everyone is correct. You tell yourself that you are a fraud, and the truth will be revealed at any moment. I know exactly how that feels.

Do you know what I did, and still do, to silence that little voice that tells me I'm a fraud? Every time I was writing a new chapter of my journey, I increased the volume of my self-esteem, took a deep breath, lifted my head, and went for it. I still do this today. I force myself to remember my skills, the things I'm good at, and everything that made me get to where I am instead of focusing on my weaknesses and limitations. I also tell the impostor's voice to get out of my head because I don't have time for it. Validating yourself and working on your self-esteem daily makes all the difference so you can be who you want to be with your head held high.

Do you think you're the only one experiencing this? Unfortunately, not! Even Michelle Obama, the former first lady of the United States and a well-connected, politicized, wonderful woman, declared that she suffers from this syndrome. On a visit to a school in London, Michelle admitted to questioning her skills and feeling insecure in many situations. Can you believe it?

The singer Jennifer Lopez shared that despite selling 70 million records, she didn't feel good about what she does. Sheryl Sandberg, Chief Operating Officer of Facebook, said that not too long ago she'd wake feeling like a fraud and wasn't sure if she belonged where she was. In other words, imposter syndrome can strike when you are on the rise at any point during your career. You may often feel that you are not capable enough. You might even believe your colleagues could do a better job than you.

We were raised to lend our dolls to our friends and say "yes" to everything. We learned that speaking highly of ourselves and accepting praise is arrogance. These lessons harmed us. We were not taught to deal with power. That was always for the boys. Being allowed to rise and fall. To make mistakes and try again. To believe you are the strongest and to punch your chest to prove it. They consistently receive praise for these things. We don't. Consequently, this taught us to refuse compliments, speak in the third person about an idea we conceived, and feel like a fraud when we occupy spaces we're not usually allowed. ENOUGH! Let's redefine all of this!

Understand your feelings, value your power, and make your voice heard during meetings, on stages, and in leadership positions. You are a woman, and you are powerful. You are capable. You are not a fraud. Take possession of the powerful woman that lives inside you and take up space. And if you're scared, do it anyway!

You're NOT stuck up.
You ARE secure.

You're NOT stupid.
You ARE assertive and objective.

You are no one's mother.
You ARE a welcoming leader.

You are NOT arrogant.
You HAVE an opinion.

You are NOT selfish.
You HAVE self-love.

You are NOT ungrateful.

You ARE NOT obligated to have
eternal debts with anyone.

You're NOT antisocial.
You just DON'T TOLERATE
toxic people.

You are NOT responsible for anyone other than yourself.

You are NOT a fraud.
You HAVE value.

You're NOT nosy.
You just WANT to share your opinion.

You are NOT obligated to do anything.

You didn't get here by chance.
You and your story ARE worth so much.

YOU ARE UNIQUE.

You deserve to be where you are.

You deserve to achieve your goals.

CHAPTER 5

The Mirror Test

Mirror therapy helps us work on self-knowledge and awaken intimacy with ourselves. Embrace yourself, touch yourself, talk, cry, and laugh. Observe yourself. Question yourself. Most importantly, pay attention to your feelings.

Warning: *This exercise is not recommended for people with depression. If you experience any discomfort, seek help from a trusted psychotherapist.*

Start by grabbing a hand mirror or a full-length mirror if you have one. Choose a private spot in your home where you can be alone. Look into your eyes and gaze at yourself. If you feel like crying, cry. If you want to scream, laugh, jump, or dance, do it.

Talk to yourself. Look deeply at yourself. See yourself. Be your best friend.

Have you ever seen people who talk to themselves? I'm like that. I laugh at myself, scold myself, guide myself, and give myself advice all the time.

Start by talking to yourself. Looking into your eyes, what do you think of yourself? What do you want for yourself?

Say what you believe might upset you or what you might be doing that's getting in your way. Compliment yourself.

Who She Think She Is?
Vivi Duarte

Talk about your qualities out loud, looking at yourself in the mirror. Let yourself know what you think. It seems crazy, but it isn't. Speak with affection and embrace yourself.

We increasingly have less time to see ourselves. We look at others, and because of the rush of everyday life, we forget to look at ourselves. Don't leave yourself behind. Even on the most challenging and busy days, compliment and validate yourself in front of the mirror.

Tell yourself it doesn't matter what others say. You will continue believing in yourself and will not give up on the powerful woman you are and seek to be.

When we praise ourselves, the brain gets so excited that it releases oxytocin, the love hormone. This substance leaves us lighter, happier, and more productive. Love yourself. Be kind and honor yourself.

So shout it out loud to yourself: "You, wonderful fairy, you will achieve everything you want! I love you, and we are living this chaotic life together. No one can hold us back or put us down because we're in this together, and we will dominate the world with our goals!"

Wow, I feel my heart flutter with so much self-love!

Loving yourself above all else is what will make you achieve your goals. No strange glances, whispers, or toxic people can resist self-love.

Everyone gets out of the way, and the path is clear for you to become the amazing woman you want to be. So love yourself!

SELF-CONFIDENCE TEST

How would you respond when someone compliments you?

a) "Oh, it was nothing!"

b) You credit your success to the universe, the ecosystem, and pretty much anything else.

c) "Thank you. I also like how it turned out."

How would you respond when someone interrupts you?

a) You stay silent and move on from the topic.

b) You go back to the topic once the person has finished speaking.

c) You don't allow them to interrupt and ask to complete your thoughts.

Someone criticizes the outfit you're wearing, which you love, so you:

a) Think about changing and thank them for the tip.

b) Continue wearing the outfit, but plan on never wearing it again.

c) Decide to keep wearing the outfit because the fact that you like it is what matters.

Someone underestimates your dream, so you:

a) Agree that you're dreaming too big, and it's best to bring your feet back to the ground.

b) Give up on your dream because of someone else's opinion.

c) Feel even more motivated to make your dream come true.

Score:

a) 0.

b) 1.

c) 10.

If you failed to complete at least 20 points, it's time to improve your self-esteem and confidence so you can become the protagonist of your life. You can't let anyone influence you, not in the corporate world and much less in your personal life.

If you have completed 30 points, come with me. You'll learn how to complete 100, and no one will be able to hold you back. We're not here to be left behind! Let's go!

Who She Think She Is?
Vivi Duarte

CHAPTER 6

What Did You Want To Be When You Grew Up?

I already mentioned that I always wanted to be a journalist, right? It didn't matter where I lived nor whether or not my family could afford for me to attend college. When we are children, everything is possible. Have you noticed that?

Back in the day, there was an advertisement for juice boxes that I loved. In it, children appeared talking about their futures and what they wanted to be when they grew up. They didn't hesitate, just like I didn't when someone asked six-year-old me what I wanted to be. "Owner of an ant farm!" "Discoverer of other universes!" "Warriors against pollution!" No child was afraid of sharing their dream. None were discouraged or worried about what others would say or think. They were all accurate and authentic in talking about their plans, which has incredible value.

If you close your eyes and think about what you wanted and dreamed of when you were a young girl, many good and funny memories will come to mind. Unless you had a childhood harmed by a mediocre adult who somehow hurt you (in which case I'm sorry that happened. I'm here for you!) Otherwise, you will certainly have good memories of your childhood and your big plans.

When you are a child, no limiting factor stops you from dreaming. Your essence is there, as is the courage to achieve. Courage to believe in yourself. At this stage, children live in a bubble of comfort because they are still unaware of the system and its gender, race, and social class oppressions. That's why children dream without limits, and revisiting this place as an adult is liberating. Do this for yourself. Dream without limits because dreaming small and dreaming big takes the same amount of work. Grab your dreams and plans, and let's do this together!

UNDERSTAND THAT THE DREAM IS ONLY YOURS

I remember an older lady named Mrs. Antonia in the tenement where I spent my early childhood. I loved going to her house in the afternoons to eat cake and have coffee while listening to her stories. She was a black woman with a light smile and a peaceful gentleness.

Every time I ran into her kitchen, she calmly asked me to clean my shoes on the carpet. So, I'd slow down and enjoy the sweet smell from the stove. It was either pumpkin candy, orange peels, rice pudding, or hominy.

Mrs. Antônia never disappointed, but I remember the first time that I realized that people would never please us all the time. I was telling Mrs. Antônia about my dreams and that I would become a journalist. With a hairbrush, I simulated a microphone and started to interview her. She looked at me with a worried and serious expression and said, "My child, your dream will never happen. It's impossible. Look at your family's conditions and understand that so you won't get hurt. Those who dream big have an even bigger fall."

I was shocked by the invalidation coming from a woman I adored, and who had a good heart. I was sure of that. I kept thinking about how she dared to tell me that without blinking. I almost believed her. So I went home and told my mother, who, like a good mentor, said to me, "Whose dream is it? *Yours!* So it only depends on *you* to make it happen. Stop listening to those who don't believe in you. A lot of people believe, and those are the people that matter. But *you* are the one who matters most. Do you believe it? So that's that!"

Learning to free your dreams, like when you were a child, and not listening to pessimists will make you achieve your goals.

Pessimists can be people we love but who have stopped dreaming. They may have stopped dreaming out of fear of taking risks because of many obstacles and struggles without victory or because their experiences have limited them. Don't judge them. Just follow your journey while understanding that the dream is yours and that it will depend on you to make it come true.

I matured very early because I had to strengthen myself as an older sister to help my mother at home with my little sister and brother. I took care of them so my mother could work, and at 14 years old, I officially started working.

Vivi Duarte

My mom got me a job at a household items store on a commercial street in *Lapa*, São Paulo. I did everything. I helped the saleswomen and worked in the stock room, package department, and administrative side. That's where I learned how to deal with all kinds of people, and I would attentively observe how the saleswomen differed from each other. How they'd sell more or less depends on their ability and willingness to show and offer products to customers. Some did not understand the customer's profile and offered them products that weren't a fit. Others examined the consumer to understand their taste and what they were looking for. I thought it was magical when a customer bought more than they initially wanted. Sometimes, a person would come into the store to buy a set of glasses and leave with a complete dinnerware set and decorative objects. I fell in love with it. Selling became something more profound to me. It was always in my DNA, with a father who was a salesman and a peddler, and a mother and grandmother who were vendors from the *Brás*. I had the salesperson gene, and just needed to perfect that skill.

I soon resigned from the store, and at 15, I went to work as a saleswoman at a clothing store called *Canal 27*. I was part of a sales team that had to organize themselves to serve the customers. When it was your turn to sell, you had to identify what the customer was looking for and what else could be offered without scaring them away. You also couldn't demonstrate the importance of the sale in reaching your monthly or daily sales goal. You had to have nerves of steel, emotional intelligence, and transparency. For example, I never lied to a client, saying they looked great in an outfit if I thought otherwise. This built a relationship of trust which helped me gain a loyal customer base who always sought me out and made it a point to only shop with me. I thought that was incredible! Transparency in relationships is everything. It contributes to a good reputation and adds value regardless of the context or where you are working.

ARE YOU A GOOD SALESWOMAN?

If there's one thing I realized early on, it's that learning to sell makes you agile in many ways. Regardless of the circumstances, you have to know how to sell. Be it a product or an idea. Selling your brand, selling yourself at a job interview, or on social media if you want to build a reputation as an influencer in your field. We need to learn how to use sales tools to our advantage. If this isn't an ability you have, you need to practice. Selling needs to be within the technical skills of someone who has a plan and wants to get it off the ground. Don't be ashamed. Encourage yourself and learn.

Tips for exercising your skills as a salesperson

Forget prejudice

You can be an entrepreneur with incredible ideas and focus all your efforts on creation and innovation, but no one knows how to value your brand or business's attributes better than you. So, create a script with everything you identify as special, highlighting your business's competitive differences, image, and journey to enhance its value in the market. Use this to your advantage when negotiating everything, from creating content for your communication channels to pricing your service or product.

Practice your presentation with your friends or your team.

Prepare slides that build an objective narrative that answers the following questions:

- **What:** What is your idea or business about?
- **How:** How can this idea or business solve a problem or meet a demand?
- **Where:** On what channels is this business present?
- **Why:** Tell us why this business is worth it and makes sense, explaining its uniqueness and potential.
- **For whom:** Who is your business's target audience?

Benchmark first!

Look at major competitors or businesses similar to yours and study each one. What are they missing? What can you do to make your company differentiate itself with added value and purpose?

Schedule business meetings or coffees with potential clients

Introduce yourself, your business, and your ideas. Listen to feedback and understand how the market and potential customers perceive you and your business. Adapt what you consider relevant, review your sales script, and move forward.

INTRAPRENEURS

I had my professional start in retail, specifically in shopping mall fashion stores in São Paulo. I was a manager and salesperson responsible for stores such as *Canal 27, Khelf, Arezzo, MOB* (formerly Mó Bethat), *Forum,* and *Triton.* I worked from 10 AM to 10 PM, and on the weekends, I'd eat quickly in the stock room so I wouldn't miss out on any business. I always hit my sales goals. My personal ones. I never started a job to meet the company's stipulations but to fulfill my plans and reach my goals, which were generally more ambitious.

I felt like the owner of where I worked and did everything I could to stand out at each of them. At the time, I needed to save money for college, extracurricular courses, and help around the house. My big plans depended on me. From the beginning, the "intrapreneurship" mindset helped me look at the business world with a magnitude beyond the employee versus company relationship. Most importantly, I always had space to act as an intrapreneur within the companies I worked for. That always brought excellent results for me, the team, and the entire company.

Intrapreneurship comes from the expression "intrapreneur," which means the movement of an individual who can take an entrepreneurial role within the company they work for. Intra-corporate entrepreneurship is currently highly valued by companies that seek innovations and talent who identify as business owners.

How about giving intrapreneurship a try?

You can sell your ideas internally (within the company you work for) without having to give up your executive career to make it happen. Entrepreneurship and starting a business rely on several factors and skills. Many people do not have the psychological, physical, and financial preparation to afford this game. There are millions of entrepreneurs in Brazil, but it is important to understand the circumstances and the annual income of these women who gave up their careers to become entrepreneurs.

Many were catapulted out of the corporate world after returning from maternity leave and had no other option. Others have financial privileges that allowed them to venture into the entrepreneurial world. If nothing works out, they can take a sabbatical year in India and start a new role at a multinational company when they return.

However, most Brazilian entrepreneurs work 24 hours a day, seven days a week. They sleep thinking about the bills, payroll, taxes, customers they're running late on, and employees who don't perform well. It's a world of challenges that are irrelevant to you. So before resigning, analyze everything around you. Is there room in your company for you to become an intrapreneur? Is it possible for you to lead projects with purpose that result in your professional advancement? Can you create a side project that allows you to get a taste of the entrepreneurial world before diving in? How many months would you be able to support yourself financially if you resigned and started your business, considering that every company needs at least two years of investment to generate profit and return?

You need to answer all these questions so you don't fall into the ditch that leads many women to depression and makes them lose everything.

"Stage entrepreneurship" does not show you the behind-the-scenes. Many internet experts don't even own a company. They are good public speakers. So, put your feet on the ground and analyze everything around you, especially if you have a good-paying job. After all, even in the world of entrepreneurship, there are numerous challenges, sexism, harassment, and opportunism.

If you commit to entrepreneurship, be aware of all of this. Don't fall for an old wives' tale. I have mentored many lost women who left their careers and who did not have the profile to handle the demands that an entrepreneur in Brazil carries. I don't want to pour cold water on anyone. This is my way of helping you work with your reality and think carefully about which scenario you are willing to act upon. Whatever it is, count on me and the *Plano Feminino* (Feminine Plan). We're in this together!

Who She Think She Is?
Vivi Duarte

CHAPTER 7

My Timeline

MARRIED AT 16, WHAT NOW?

The moment I put the timeline of my life into perspective, I felt stuck while writing this book. Today, I have a business that focuses on creating new advertisement narratives so women are not stereotyped. I created an institute, *Plano de Menina* (Girl Plan), to enable girls from the outskirts of Brazil to be protagonists of their stories and break the patterns and statistics of marriage and adolescent pregnancy. I was one of them.

At 16, I was already a salesperson at a mall. I had endured many floods and was in my last year of high school. I felt like a mature woman. Due to the lack of privileges, I had to mature quickly. Coming from a low-income family meant having to take care of the house and my siblings while seeing our parents fight to support us, often unsuccessfully. At 16, I already had so many stories to tell. Girls from poor families get married early, and I never stopped to think about how I was part of this shameful statistic that exists in Brazil and around the world.

According to UNICEF, roughly 650 million women worldwide were married before the end of adolescence.

I was a part of this statistic.
One in every five girls gets married
before they turn 18.
That's 23 girls every minute.

Who She Think She Is?
Vivi Duarte

According to data from research released by the Girls Not Brides Institution, girls from poor families are three times more likely to get married before the age of 18 than girls from wealthier families. According to data reported by the NGO Save The Children, Brazil is the worst country in South America to be born a woman. The report evaluated 144 nations, and Brazil is ranked 103 on the Opportunities for Girls index, standing out as one of the countries that most deprive women of opportunities, preventing them from having the means and self-esteem to succeed.

Back to my story, I wasn't pregnant. I was in love. I was in love with my husband (I was married for 25 years), and I was in love with the possibility of more independence, autonomy, and a new life built from our efforts and commitment. He had a better socioeconomic status than me and was only 18 years old. Who, in good conscience, marries at that age with the privileges that boy had? And me? Who authorizes a 16-year-old girl with a fiery passion to get married? You can't blame anyone. The adults around us had the same record. Therefore, there was a climate of support and normalization of the scenario. My mother cried because she disagreed and said, "Don't stop studying. Be independent of men."

My father signed the papers at the registry office in silence. He had already said he disagreed with what we were doing, but he authorized it anyway. There was a party atmosphere with huge questions looming: Is she pregnant? How long will this last? Months went by, and no baby arrived.

We got married because we wanted to be close to each other, and I felt protected by him (yes, I was 16 years old!). Everything was new, and I sometimes missed my mother's arms, her cooking, the smell of my bed, and even my siblings and our fights. I missed how my mother would get annoyed at my father at the dinner table for taking a massive scoop of food from the middle of the dish, ruining the aesthetic of the meal. I cried in secret. What stopped me from succumbing to my predetermined fate was that my ex-husband had always been a partner. This helped me a lot.

DON'T LEAVE ME BEHIND

One of the things that saved me in that marriage was the clarity I had on who I was and where I wanted to go. It was essential to make it clear that I was married because I loved him, but that I loved The Woman I dreamed of being even more and was fighting for her. I was very privileged that I didn't become another statistic. The one where women who get married, especially at this age, have their plans invalidated by their husbands and are abused every time they demonstrate any autonomy and protagonism. Brazil is the fifth country with the highest feminicide (femicide) rate in the world. The lack of independence contributes to women becoming hostages in abusive relationships. They give up on their plans without any strength to leave the relationship.

How many women have lost their goals, their lives, their self-esteem, and their entire world to sexist men? How many are invalidated and are obligated to serve and coexist every day of their lives?

I am an exception. However, getting married at 16 took away many important things from me—many stories and experiences. I can't romanticize this part of my life because getting married at 16 is abnormal. I will fight for no girl to follow this path before knowing herself, empowering herself, and acquiring financial and emotional autonomy. When these statistics change, more and more girls will become leaders in their personal and professional lives.

It's surreal to realize that I built my legacy and the business models of *Plano Feminino* and *Plano de Menina Institute* (Girl Plan), focusing on freeing girls and women from the social standards and pressures I experienced. It's as if, consciously and unconsciously, every step in my journey was a battle cry for myself and all of us.

At 21, I became the mother of a beautiful boy, Paulo Neto. I had been married for five years and had a head full of plans. But what would I do now?

CAN A MOTHER HAVE GOALS?

At 21, I discovered that being a mother in the corporate world was like having a contagious and fatal virus. I was looking to relocate as a salesperson, telemarketing operator, receptionist, or whatever I could manage to pay for school and the bills. And all I heard in the job interviews were:

"Why did you marry so young?"

"Why did you have a child so early?"

"How many children do you intend to have by 30?"

"Who will take care of your child?"

"How will you study and work if you are a mother?"

"How will you be able to travel for work?"

"Did you accidentally get pregnant?"

"Didn't you use a condom?"

Who She Think She Is?
Vivi Duarte

Yes, these questions and others that were even more awkward were asked by men and women who interviewed me for job openings. I felt the nausea, fear, and stress run through my body and send shivers down my spine. I wanted to cry and, at the same time, had a knot in my throat that made me answer each question with a tight voice.

I focused only on the judgmental looks and forgot about my power and everything I was capable of and had already accomplished until then.

The recruitment company CATHO conducted research that shows the reality of women in the job market after the arrival of children. After becoming mothers, they leave the job market five times more often than men. The company surveyed 13,161 people and concluded that 28% of women interviewed left their jobs after becoming mothers, compared to 5% of men. Research also shows that 21% of women take more than three years to return to the job market, compared to 2% of men in the same situation.

Do they ask men if they care about their homes and children in job interviews?

I left those interviews feeling devastated. From that moment on, I think a feminist was born without me knowing.

HAVING KIDS ENHANCES OUR SKILLS

According to an experiment from the University of Richmond, having children makes women smarter. The research showed that laboratory mice became excellent hunters after giving birth. The ones who had never been mothers took, on average, 270 seconds to hunt for a cricket hidden in a maze. Those who had already given birth to their babies were five times sharper; they found the cricket in fifty seconds.

Another experiment by the same group, led by American psychologist Craig Kinsley, showed that rodent mothers are calmer than the maidens. In stressful situations, they showed less neuronal activity in their limbic system, the area of the brain that triggers fear and anxiety. In other words, besides being smart, the rats were more focused after having children. It is known that for us humans, the brain loses 7% of its mass during pregnancy. However, as soon as the baby is born, the gray mass returns to normal, and with an upgrade, there are more connections between neurons. We increase our ability to decipher feelings and increase our interpersonal relationship power.

Pay close attention to these numbers. And if you are a mother in a situation where you are coerced to prove that being a mother will not hinder your performance, respond confidently and with a scientific basis. Being a mother only enhanced your soft skills and made you even more remarkable.

Vivi Duarte

But it was the 2000s, and I wore those hideous bras with silicone straps that burned the skin when exposed to the sun, low-waisted pants (which always left the butt exposed), cropped boleros, and listened to everything from *Evanescence* to *Banda Cine*.

I had no idea what feminism was. Nor racism. I had no idea what sexism or misogyny was either. I just felt nauseous every time I was subjected to job interviews and forced to expose myself. I left the interview room feeling like nothing because I was a mother who had married early and had no relevant familial experience in the market. No one in my family was a CEO or had a role that could be helpful during the conversation. I didn't collect international trips on my resume; I was just starting college.

Who was I?

I saw this question mark on the foreheads of some interviewers when I dared to say how good, focused, professional, and ready I was for the job. *Who are you, sweetheart?*

But there was something that none of those people could take away from me. My self-esteem and genuine stubbornness to believe in who I was and wanted to become. I turned the nausea into indignation, and that indignation in strength. I'll tell you how.

TAKE THIS FOR YOURSELF

For those of you who, like me, didn't know any of the following terms but lived them all daily and suffocated themselves, learn and share with other women. Ignorance blinds and suffocates us.

We need to understand our society and each of these words. They are loaded with struggle, oppression, and significance. By understanding them in depth, we will have more conditions to fight for our rights and the women we want to become daily.

Feminist

If you believe in social, political, economic, and sexual equality between genders and that women deserve to have the same rights as men, guess what:

YOU ARE A FEMINIST.

> "I have always been a feminist. This means I oppose discrimination of women in all forms of gender-based inequality, but it also means that I demand a policy that considers restrictions imposed by gender on human development." - **Judith Butler**

Black Feminist

When we talk about gender equality and fight for more women in leadership positions, for the rights of women to earn the same salaries, among other issues, we are obviously not talking about black women who, in Brazil, are at the base of the pyramid and is the one who suffers most from gender and racial issues.

Black feminism is a segment of feminism that fights for urgent issues for black women so that they have visibility and a voice in society.

"The invisibility of black women within the feminist agenda means that they don't even have their problems identified. And no one thinks of emancipatory solutions to problems that were not even mentioned."
- Djamila Ribeiro

"Feminism is the radical notion that women are human beings." - **Cheris Kramarae**

"The prejudiced bark, but the caravan passes." - **Maju Coutinho**

Machismo

Machismo is based on the devaluation of women in society, underestimating her capacity for personal, professional, and sexual achievements just because she is a woman. Machismo positions men as superior beings, believing that women should play the role of submission and subservience. In machismo, women do not have the right to be free in their choices, and when they are, they are judged, stereotyped, and sexualized.

Racism

Racism is prejudice and discrimination based on biological differences between people, such as race and ethnicity.

> "I was raised to believe that excellence is the best deterrent to racism or sexism. And that's how I operate my life."
> - **Oprah**

Antiracist

Being anti-racist means fighting against racism in all its forms, spaces, and demonstrations. It is about recognizing your privileges and fighting to reverse the social pyramid of oppression.

"In a racist society, it is not enough to be non-racist; we must be anti-racist."
- **Angela Davis**

Sexism

Sexism most often affects girls and women. This is discrimination based on a person's gender or sex.

Some people felt I should talk about my personal struggle in order to shed a spotlight on the greater issue. Maybe I'm being presumptuous, but I assumed it was obvious that women in all positions struggle for equality. It's always an uphill battle and fight. My experience with my close female friends and family is that the struggle is real for everybody. Everyone has been discriminated against or harassed—sexism is real."
- **Scarlett Johansson**

Misogyny

Misogyny is the act of contempt for women and girls that can be manifested in various ways, such as sexual objectification, sexual discrimination, social exclusion, and hostility, among other acts that diminish, hurt, and make women invisible.

> "Feminism is hated because women are hated. Antifeminism is a direct expression of misogyny; it is the political defense of woman hating." - **Andrea Dworkin**

Xenophobia

Xenophobia is the aversion to people who come from a different country with different cultures, habits, races, or religions.

> The only way to overcome xenophobia is through language. Spontaneously, we like what is similar. To like something different, you have to listen to it.
> - **Betty Milan**

Homophobia

Homophobia is the aversion towards homosexual people, bisexuals, and, in some cases, transgender and intersex people.

> The reason why intolerance, sexism, racism,
> and homophobia exist is because of fear.
> People are afraid of their own feelings
> and the unknown.
> -   **Madonna**

Fatphobia

It is the aversion to fat and people who are overweight, making them feel inferior to others. The term comes into play to identify the prejudice that fat people suffer in their emotional, social, and professional lives.

> "We are talking about access. A fat person
> doesn't find clothes with ease, doesn't fit in
> chairs, and doesn't fit on the plane, among
> other distressing everyday situations."
> - **Alexandra Gurgel**

Who She Think She Is?

Vivi Duarte

Take the following quiz.

ARE YOU A FEMINIST?

( ) Do you believe that women and men need to have the same rights?

( ) Do you agree that women earn 30% less than men exercising the same role?

( ) Do you think it is normal for a woman to be invalidated in the job market because she is a woman or a mother?

( ) Do you think it is normal for women to be harassed for their clothes or because of their existence?

( ) Do you agree that men need to share household chores with women?

If you ticked off the first question, you are already a feminist. Do your research, and don't believe fake news. Get informed and fight for your rights and those of other women. Use your privileges to help other women to carry out their goals.

Who She Think She Is?
Vivi Duarte

CHAPTER 8

Get Ready To Hack The System

IN YOUR FAMILY AND SOCIETY

When you discover yourself as a feminist, it's like an "anti-scam radar" settles in your mind. You will never be the same again. The penny drops and everything starts to make sense when you discover all the suffocation, chest tightness, sleepless nights, irritation at family dinners, and accusations that you are crazy are connected.

You know when your husband or wife or partner doesn't share the house chores with you and leaves you feeling overwhelmed and guilty (after all, you are the head of the house), saying, "Wow, this house is a mess! You need to organize your time better?"

You know when that relative sees you traveling for your job and pokes fun at your marriage by saying, "Those who don't assist make room for competition?"

You know when that co-worker finds out you will represent the company on a trip and immediately says, "But who's going to look after your children?"

In these types of situations, you realize that all these provocations, whether conscious or not, are the result of a sexist and patriarchal society that insists on imposing on us the role of "beautiful, modest, and homely."

Vivi Duarte

In the text "The Angel in the House" from the 1930s, Virginia Woolf talks about the agony of being a woman full of plans and dealing with the conception of women that society wanted to fit her into. She says that while writing the piece, she killed the idea of the "angel in the house" who insisted on imprisoning her:

"And while I was writing that review, I discovered that if I were going to review books I would need to do battle with a certain phantom. And the phantom was a woman, and when I came to know her better I called her after the heroine of a famous poem, The Angel in the House. It was she who used to come between me and my paper when I was writing reviews. It was she who bothered me and wasted my time and so tormented me that at last I killed her. You who come from a younger and happier generation may not have heard of her—you may not know what I mean by the Angel in the House. I will describe her as shortly as I can. She was intensely sympathetic. She was immensely charming. She was utterly unselfish. She excelled in the difficult arts of family life. She sacrificed herself daily. If there was chicken, she took the leg; if there was a draught she sat in it—in short, she was so constituted that she never had a mind or a wish of her own, but preferred to sympathize always with the minds and wishes of others. Above all—I need not say it—she was pure. Her purity was supposed to be her chief beauty—her blushes, her great grace. In those days—the last of Queen Victoria—every house had its Angel. And when I came to write I encountered her with the very first words. The shadow of her wings fell on my page; I heard the rustling of her skirts in the room. Directly, that is to say, I took my pen in my hand to review that novel by a famous man, she slipped behind me and whispered: "My dear, you are a young woman. You are writing about a book that has been written by a man. Be sympathetic; be tender; flatter; deceive; use all the arts and wiles of our sex. Never let anybody guess that you have a mind of your own. Above all, be pure." (Excerpt from WOOLF, Virginia. *The Death of the Moth, and Other Essays*).

You must understand the game of machismo and patriarchy, look around and recalculate your route. We deserve relationships and spaces where we can share tasks and happy moments, be respected, and feel valued. And these spaces exist. These people exist. Don't diminish yourself to fit into anyone's mediocre and sexist life.

To hack the system and become the leader of your life, you need to identify toxic people and clean them out. That can mean ending relationships or giving them new meaning as a woman aware of her power and who she wants to become. It is essential that you know what you deserve, or you'll experience the oppressive movements and imprisonments firsthand. Never let anything or anyone put you in boxes. You were born to be free from standards and the author of your own story.

Becoming a feminist is painful and more intense, depending on where you're coming from and the social class in which you are placed. If you are a woman with financial autonomy, freedom from abusive relationships, and mental balance, it will be easier. But if you are an outskirt woman, who lives in an abusive relationship and depends financially and emotionally on someone, you will need a lot of strategy, effort, and a support network to get out of this place and fly free as you deserve. Seek support, create a network of allies, and try to establish yourself financially in some way so you can take action. Regardless of social class, if you suffer any type of violence, physical or psychological, report it immediately. Run away. Don't wait.

Pressures of being a woman, mother, and executive

After facing bizarre interviews and finally managing to become an executive, I had to face even greater pressure.

When I started working in a marketing position, I had to travel a lot.

I lived "out of a suitcase." That was the expression that some family members and friends liked to say to me to remind me that I had a family, and from their perspective, I was being careless. People would always tell me, "This isn't a married woman's job. Be careful with your husband, okay?" "Your home is the road, right?" "What does your husband think of all this?" "If I were your husband, you wouldn't be like this," "Poor children, being cared for by their father." This kind of opinion made me feel the burden of packing my bags when I needed to travel, practically every week. In those moments, I felt terrible and thought I was wronging my husband, who was always my friend and partner. Worst of all, I felt I was abandoning my son out of selfishness. After all, why did I want a successful career so much? I left with a heavy conscience and cried when I arrived at the airport.

But when the plane took off, I looked at the sky and the clouds that looked like cotton candy and remembered my childhood dream of being The Woman I was becoming. Then I stopped crying and thought, "Everything is fine. We are fine, and we are succeeding in being The Woman we always dreamed of being."

Have you noticed that when we return to our essence, purpose, and mission to be who we want to be, no type of oppression or judgment can stop us?

Try this out for yourself. Whenever you're in a situation that makes you doubt who you are and what you are doing, go back and look at your dream, plan, and why, and the answer will come. You don't have to live with the guilt of being The Woman who dreams of being the protagonist of her story. Get rid of that guilt and focus on your plan.

Don't blame yourself, don't blame yourself,
don't blame yourself, don't blame yourself,
don't blame yourself, don't blame yourself,
don't blame yourself, don't blame yourself,
don't blame yourself, don't blame yourself,
don't blame yourself, don't blame yourself,
blame yourself, don't blame yourself, don't
blame yourself, don't blame yourself, don't
blame yourself, don't blame yourself, don't
blame yourself, don't blame yourself, don't
blame yourself, don't blame yourself, don't
blame yourself blame, don't blame yourself,
don't blame yourself, don't blame yourself,
don't blame yourself, don't blame yourself,
don't blame yourself, don't blame yourself,
don't blame yourself, don't blame yourself,
don't blame yourself, don't blame yourself,
don't blame yourself, don't blame yourself.
DON'T BLAME YOURSELF.

IN SEARCH OF A JOB OR CLIENTS

Knowing your value and main skills (the ones that make you stand out the most) is extremely important for gaining clients or a good position. Remember what we said about knowing how to sell your ideas and learning how to do this by building a powerful narrative? This technique is called storytelling and storydoing and is used in various scenarios, especially in advertising and marketing.

Storytelling is the ability to tell stories using engaging narrative techniques and audiovisual resources. You can build your story by creatively highlighting your leading powers and technical and emotional skills so that people understand and connect more effectively with you.

Storydoing is the technique of putting storytelling into action, delivering greater connection and values backed by your brand. After all, better than telling a good story is making it happen!

The idea here is that you use these techniques to present your professional journey, highlighting your technical and emotional skills. Put together a storyboard and create a mental map of this script so that you are proficient at telling your story.

We are constantly self-sabotaging. We've already talked about impostor syndrome and how much it prevents us from achieving, right? So enough!

IN THE NETWORKING WORLD

I remember the first time I used Facebook and Twitter (I hadn't even heard of LinkedIn then) to connect with professionals I admired and wanted to have coffee with to discuss our goals. The year was 2008. After many years in the corporate world, I was overloaded and wanted new possibilities to expand my knowledge and contact network. I thought Facebook was great for networking. For as long as we've been on this earth, men network, which is nothing more than establishing work contacts and making connections based on professional interests, to develop a win-win relationship. But when we women enter the game, everything changes. Our bodies are often seen as a bargain.

In an attempt to make several professional contacts, as much as I established a narrative highly focused on business, it was poorly interpreted. I often received invitations to dinners to "get to know each other better." We women need to have the stomach to hack the sexist system of the patriarchal structure in which we live. We need to know who we are and never back down.

There are several surveys and testimonials from women reporting the harassment they suffered in the corporate environment, especially on platforms such as LinkedIn. Generally, they come from men who insist on transforming work and business connections into "dates." Say no without blinking.

I have always dealt with this type of situation in a straightforward way by calling out what was happening, "I'm here to talk business, and you are harassing me! Do you find this funny or normal? Would you like it to happen to you? If you continue, I will have to report you!" I'd lose out on business contacts, but not my dignity. I never backed down. It didn't intimidate me. I'd just continue looking for new contacts.

Depending on your business model and career, you can use LinkedIn and other platforms to connect with interesting and inspiring people who share your purposes.

For example, I made a list of ten women I wanted to get to know. They inspired me a lot, so I contacted each of them through social media to share my idea of creating the *Plano Feminino*. Three of them are my friends today. They were already CEOs of their companies while I was still building myself up. So, don't be afraid to network. Build your network based on your truth and your plans.

IN THE ENTREPRENEURSHIP WORLD

Never start a business without first calculating all the risks and opportunities. Create your own goals, and never compare yourself to others. Create a network of suppliers and partners with an aligned purpose. Never be afraid or let your ego stop you from making decisions. If you need to retreat, retreat. If you need to give up, give up and start again.

Vivi Duarte

When you enter the game, be prepared for anything. Have a cash flow that helps you to have the confidence to start. I didn't have much, and I lost a lot of money making decisions and forming the wrong partnerships, which made me retreat numerous times and practically fail. If possible, before starting a company, create business partnerships to get a feel for people's work.

Keep an eye on everything within your company. Be present and let people know who owns the business without fear of coming off as arrogant. I often overlooked the importance of taking the reins and making a name for myself within the company to please employees and partners. I thought it sounded arrogant to say I was the CEO of my own company despite having created it alone and having planned and invested with so much blood, sweat, and tears. Sometimes, we believe that giving up our truth for the sake of what others will feel is easier and more comfortable, but it's not. Make your hierarchical position, story, and commitment to your company clear. Define employee roles, including those who can or cannot be spokespeople.

When starting, we tend not to pay attention to the essential details that define the enterprise's territory, values, and reputation. Build your company and personal brand based on the purpose you created it with. Show your face to the market and remember to sell. Without that, nothing works.

Put it all into contracts. Trust me. We do a lot of stupid things when we get excited.

SWOT

SWOT analysis is a tool for mapping the internal and external factors that interact positively or negatively with your company. It comprises four elements: Strengths, Weaknesses, Opportunities, and Threats.

- **Strengths:** What makes you stand out in the market compared to your competition?
- **Weaknesses:** What factors prevent you from moving forward?
- **Opportunities:** What do you do best that can make your company more competitive?
- **Threats:** What are the internal and external factors that can hinder you?

AT A NEW ROLE IN THE COMPANY

When you get a promotion, your little self-sabotage voice makes you think that at any moment you will be caught for not having the necessary skills to occupy that position. You'll believe better professionals could be in your place or your language skills aren't good enough. We've all been there, right?

To hold leadership positions, you need to work on your emotional skills, which are called soft skills, but I always say they are power skills. You can train and improve your technical skills, but if you don't have emotional intelligence and self-esteem, you will always listen to the little voice that diminishes you.

Start believing in who you are and your story. It has value. Each learning experience was worth it and transformed you into this remarkable woman. Believe and send that little voice away. Appreciate all the good you have and go for it without fear. If you get scared, do it anyway.

When I received my first promotions in the companies where I worked, I feared failing. Fearful of not getting the job done. Afraid of meetings in English because I didn't speak it as well as my peers, and I constantly compared myself. This prevented me from being heard and positioning myself better, even with the great ideas and strategies I brought to the company. Ultimately, they were stolen by my peers who had self-confidence and listened to me whisper the ideas and simply reproduced them. Has this ever happened to you?

One day, I decided this would no longer happen, and I went to the meeting prepared to raise my voice and speak in English as best I could but not give up on myself. And it worked!

My team and superintendent praised me. I felt confident and never let anyone interrupt me or take my ideas. I didn't back away even when the little voice of insecurity came in.

Being a leader also involves listening to the people on your team and preparing professionals for a possible succession in a few years. A leader does not oppress their team. Do not be afraid of talented people under your leadership. Support and use them to optimize processes and deliveries. Support your team. Think about diversity when hiring, and be a bridge for talents to connect and generate excellent results.

CHAPTER 9

Build Your Network Of Goal Accomplices

Who She Think She Is?
Vivi Duarte

I'll continue telling you about my childhood and the hurdles we had to overcome to carry out our plans. A few years later, I realized that each learning experience in that turmoil contributed to my becoming The Woman I am today.

If you look carefully at the hurdles you've overcome in your life, you will realize that everything contributed to you either becoming a powerful woman or destroyed by resentment. Only we can determine which one. I could have only held on to the scenes from my childhood where I saw my mother and grandmother desperate, without money to pay the rent. I could talk about the days when we didn't have enough food. However, I preferred to focus on the solutions I saw those women find for each situation. As mentioned, I learned to understand the power of building a support network early on.

Remember: "Those who have friends have everything!" That was my grandmother's favorite phrase. She knew, like no one else, how to form a network and have accomplices to her plans. Whether it was with her client portfolio, who never let her down and always purchased her sweets and cakes. Or the owners of our neighborhood stores, who never refused to split her payments.

Trust – Respect – Word – Integrity – Admiration – Ethics

These are the keywords that guide the construction of a network of accomplices. My grandmother and mother had this network of customers, suppliers, and fans because they kept their word. They paid as soon as they could. They respected their customers by always selling the best product. They charged a fair price for their services which was the same for everyone.

Their professionalism and integrity earned them admiration and inspired everyone around them. We need to be authentic and honest with people to create a network of accomplices. My mother and grandmother could've waited to pay back the neighborhood store when they had more money from the goods they sold, but they honored their word which generated trust.

They could sell low-quality products and use low-quality ingredients, but that was never an option because they respected their customers. They could charge each person a different price. The internet didn't exist then, and their client's neighborhoods were far from each other. They were aware of which client could pay more or less than the other and, therefore, could charge a different price. But that would compromise their integrity, which was a non-negotiable. I grew up watching these two women always figuring things out and learning that there was always a way out. These were the prominent flashbacks I kept in mind.

Who She Think She Is?
Vivi Duarte

In 2009, I was well-positioned in a health company. I was an integrated communications supervisor and managed a team. My salary was good, and I had a path to success. But I wanted to study because I saw opportunities in a very prejudiced market. So, I decided to get an MBA because I believed that the advertising model of that time was doomed to failure. I believed that our bodies wouldn't forever be objectified to sell beer or any other product. The research at the time showed that 80% of the purchasing decision power was in the hands of women, so it was time to look at things differently.

I idealized that advertisements would start considering the insertion of black women and men without, for example, carrying poverty stereotypes to sell food baskets. I also wanted women to stop being visual snacks, attracting the sale of beer with their bodies served on a tray for men to enjoy while drinking.

During my MBA, I created my first business, *Plano Feminino*, which completed ten years in 2020. It is a consultancy for brands that focuses on gender and race to make women the protagonists of new narratives, giving new meaning to stereotypes and standards that make real women invisible. Advertising and the media have always presented the same beauty standards: white, thin, straight-haired, and tall, all in a submissive role of being in the passenger seat.

I encouraged advertisements to start a dialogue of inclusion and visibility for all. We can drink beer and be the protagonist of a campaign. We can drive and do it masterfully.

We are not just the person sitting in the passenger seat! We are not just breasts and butts or snacks to add to alcohol campaigns. And we don't deserve articles that imprison us but free us.

With this encouragement, I put my creative idea at the forefront and began to build my own business alongside my work. I no longer wanted to continue at my job, but I continued to work, delivering incredible results for the company because I was committed and honored our brand! A marketing director actually started persecuting me after I launched my company. The atmosphere became heavy, but I continued.

Through *Plano Feminino*, I wanted to prove that there was no such thing as a "poetic license" to be sexist, racist, homophobic, and diminish people. I wanted to prove to the market that it was worth talking directly to us women. In addition to the purchasing power in our hands, we are the majority in universities today. We are real, and we deserve and demand a voice.

When designing my company's business model, I realized that it was robust, given the money needed, and that I would need a network of accomplices to get the company off its feet.

The first thing I remembered was the networking example I learned from the women in my house. I started drafting and analyzing who would be the accomplices of my business. I sought the best people in IT, design, content, and marketing. I told each of them about my project with the same passion my grandmother had while counting the number of ingredients she had in her *coxinha,* or cake recipe. I was the official owner of that project, and I needed to sell my baby and prove how important it was to the world. So, I prepared a presentation about *Plano Feminino* and its business fronts, which involved consultancy, education, and content. This presentation also contained figures on the market and showed my strengths and opportunities, demonstrating that it was a business with purpose and that it differentiated itself in the market. I managed to build a network of allies!

I didn't have the financial means to pay for a big development team. However, I could do exchanges, offering my expertise in marketing so that each professional involved in my project could improve their brand and make their products more sophisticated through my consultancy. We exchanged expertise, and from there, we established a format for making things happen that did not depend on money but on trust and cooperation. We put my website up, and in less than thirty days, we were already on national media talking about *Plano Feminino*.

Our network of accomplices worked like an orchestra, and I needed to figure out what to do with my 9-5 job. Yes, I built the entirety of *Plano Feminino* in the early mornings and on weekends. After all, I couldn't compromise my work and the results of my management at the company for something that was still coming to fruition.

CHAPTER 10

Successfully Fired

I didn't have to work much to resolve my employment versus entrepreneurship dilemma.

The director of the company I worked for helped me make the best decision of my life. I shared every step of my journey with her because I believed she supported my plans. I was mistaken. With each step I took in my plan, she thought about how to catapult me out of that company. Today, I laugh because I know that everything was supposed to happen this way so I could become The Woman I always dreamed of being, and today, I am. But at that time, I felt like a complete idiot. I felt stabbed in the back. Have you ever experienced this?

I remember being super excited about the start of *Plano Feminino*, and I shared a lot of the information about our achievements when I realized I was being sabotaged. Unfortunately, we women still compete a lot among ourselves. We find it extremely difficult to support each other. There is a lack of support and sisterhood. We need to discuss the scams and toxicity that we are used to experiencing due to sexism and the patriarchy. We are pitted against each other all the time, like enemies, and that is terrible.

As a sisterhood, we need to strengthen our alliances in the personal and professional world. We need to trust and support each other again. One goes up the ladder and pulls the other. Be loyal to one woman whenever you can, but obviously, always be attentive because character is not a matter of gender. On your path, there will be women who will deceive you, upset you, and make you doubt the possibility of being united, but don't give up. Stay away from toxic people and build your network of trust.

The demands at the company I worked for started to increase, and my deadline timeframes decreased despite consistently producing the best results. I delivered, even though I was forced to work late nights to meet the surreal deadlines. I eventually understood what the game was. I was pressured to give up my position and resign because I had started a business with a parallel journey. Even though it didn't compromise the company's results, that bothered me. I decided to remain in my role until the company terminated me, which happened rather quickly. I celebrated because the value of my severance package would help me invest more in my business.

Who She Think She Is?

Vivi Duarte

CHAPTER 11

Goodbye Punch Cards, Hello Entrepreneurship!

Who She Think She Is?

Vivi Duarte

I said goodbye to the corporate world and the comfort of a signed contract, confident that I would do my best never to return. I knew I needed to leave my comfort zone to overcome significant challenges. If I stayed in it, I couldn't explore my best self. We shape ourselves in the challenges and stumbles and create opportunities to achieve our big goals.

The opportunity to focus on my business 100% made all the difference. In April 2010, thirty days after launching my plan on the market, my entrepreneurial life truly began. I felt challenged but ready to use my ideas and plans to my advantage and to bring more purpose to the Brazilian advertising market.

I was focused on my business and modeling my company's products. Because things are only perfect in the world of the "stage entrepreneurs," I soon began to feel the weight of no longer having a formal contract and of having to keep my network of accomplices healthy.

Depending on customers to pay on time. Closing healthy financial deals. Paying staff. Paying expenses. Paying taxes. Paying everything. *Heeeeeelp.*

We had small customers and revenue was minimal making everyone apprehensive. Soon, disagreements began. When a company is doing poorly financially, it seems like nothing else will go well, and there is a despair that is difficult to explain. The team was tense, and what seemed like a promising business was no longer the case. I kept believing but was increasingly tense about holding on to business partners.

ONLY THOSE WHO BELIEVE STAY

Building a company from scratch and with few financial resources is quite a challenge. But the biggest one is being aware of the value of your business and having the nerves of steel to remain secure, even if everything around you is falling apart. Only those who believe stay in a company. You'll only know if you believe in your plan when things get tough and challenged to make more sudden decisions, like when faced with the possibility of returning to the job market or continuing investing in your plan.

With my partners, things were complicated. They needed money, and things were too challenging and moving. Everyone was unmotivated. When this happens, the ground falls out from underneath your feet because it seems like everything will collapse quickly. I felt very alone, even with a group of people by my side. During that period, I learned that entreprenuering is a solitary act. Only your mind is capable of idealizing and accomplishing your dreams. No matter how collaborative they are, the other people involved do not have the same feeling and passion that vibrates within you. So, it becomes easier for them to give up and move on to another project.

Vivi Duarte

It is difficult for you to realize that you made a mistake when choosing a partner or took actions and made decisions that contributed to chaos or the end of partnerships that felt so special. But that happens in the best entrepreneur families. The best decision is to end the partnership to preserve the dignity and affection that still exists before everyone gets estranged once and for all.

We never know what to expect from people regarding money and power. Never. If one day you realize that the relationship is unsustainable, both in your professional and personal life, pack up your things and end it as quickly as possible to maintain your integrity and that of those who were once important to you. That's exactly what I did.

During these ten years of entrepreneurship, I did this countless time. It's pretty challenging to find a network of accomplices and partners who have the same vibration as you and who respect your story. This does not depend exclusively on others but on yourself, too. In my ten years of experience, I understood that I could work well with my network of accomplices, but I didn't know how to deal with partners precisely because I was the creator of the entire *Plano Feminino* and because of my entrepreneurial profile, which is not open to affiliates.

I hated when people complained about the essence of my plan or criticized something. Undeniably, we all have egos and vanity. But because I valued my story and all the effort it took to build my business, I didn't want anyone telling me how things should be done. I only wanted people who believed in my vision by my side and to accompany me in putting my plans into practice. I don't know how to explain the feeling exactly, but it's like someone arriving at your home and criticizing the furniture arrangement, your pet, or your child's behavior without ever doing anything around your home. I decided only to allow myself to be criticized by people who had achieved more than me. I closed my ears to the pessimists and assumed that I was definitely a solo entrepreneur who liked partnerships but not affiliates. Knowing who you are also involves understanding what you like and don't like without judgment.

Try doing this in your life, and you will see that things make more sense. And always remember that your network needs to be built on people you admire and who admire you; otherwise, you could become their hostage. Never allow people who doubt your potential, or put themselves in a benefactor role, to invest in you or become your partners. Never put yourself in the position of receiving anyone's favor. A partnership exists to multiply expertise.

Take good care of your network and choose your allies carefully. There is nothing more destructive to the realization of a plan than relying on the wrong people. If surrounded by them, prepare your escape plan and restart the game. Go back a few houses and rebuild a healthy and trustworthy circle. It's never too late to start over. Always put everything in a contract. Formalize any and all partnerships or affiliate movements in your company, regardless of who the person is. Be aware!

Who She Think She Is?
Vivi Duarte

CHAPTER 12

What Do You Have In Your Hands?

Vivi Duarte

I remember asking my mother to let me go to concerts at Hollywood Rock, which took place in São Paulo in the 1990s and was packed with international bands. My mother always asked me, "How will you get to this concert? What's your plan?" I confess that this irritated me most of the time.

I loved the bands Guns N' Roses, Extreme, New Kids on The Block, and Skid Row. I loved the vocalists Axl Rose, Nuno, Jordan, and Sebastian Bach, and I needed to think quickly about what I could do to buy concert tickets.

Whenever my mother teased me when I asked her for something, urging me to think of a plan, I felt like screaming! I just wanted to go to the concert. I didn't want to make any plans which drove me crazy! But I knew nothing would work out if I didn't take action and have a good idea. So, I immediately thought of a plan, and it always worked! I'd buy ingredients in split payments at the store, make cakes, and sell them until I got the money. I'd then pay my supplier correctly to always count on them. Additionally, I did housework for aunts and neighbors and worked as a saleswoman on weekends in commercial stores. It always worked out, and I managed to carry out my plan stimulated by my *mamis'* powerful provocation.

How can you carry out a plan with what you have, even if that means no money? Stop seeing money as a limiting factor. It's not the most important thing for you to be able to put a plan into action. The most important thing is your ability to act and recognize your powers to make it happen, using your skills and the power of your network. There are assets more important than money, and you can create a network of assets from there.

All the lessons I learned during adolescence gave me baggage and thick skin to put myself out there and carry out my goals without backing down. What do you have available to you? What assets do you have that go beyond money?

WE'RE NEVER EMPTY-HANDED

The first years of *Plano Feminino* were turbulent: partnerships and affiliates that didn't work out, poorly invested money, debts, and a truckload of problems that left me unable to sleep properly for months. I had bet all my chips on that pot of plans, and suddenly, it seemed nothing was working. Clients didn't understand my business model. And when they understood, they told me it was crazy to challenge the market by creating communication in which they would not be sold women's breasts and butts in a beer campaign. Or they would say that real women didn't sell products and that it was insane to propose this type of communication movement in advertising. All I heard was that I needed to go back to my executive role before it was too late, and I was known as the crazy feminist who dared to challenge the advertisement market in Brazil. I only had clients with small budgets and thousands of things to deliver. It wasn't adding up.

Entrepreneurship in Brazil is a crazy challenge when your government is more like a lazy partner who only shows up on payday. Taxes are high, you don't get a return from them, and you need to earn even more money to make it worth having the great idea of starting a company. When I realized that mine was becoming a swamp monster with expired bills invading my dreams like a nightmare, I returned to my roots, reflecting on the lessons I acquired from the women in my house. I thought: "And now, with what I have available, what will my plan be?"

I confess that I was feeling quite humiliated. Sometimes, you project something but are unprepared if it doesn't go as planned. When you don't prepare to answer the question, "What if everything goes wrong?" you can end up falling into depression. That was precisely what happened to me. I encouraged myself, but I couldn't move.

I started to lose focus on my business and just look at the chaos, something I had never done before. I couldn't see a way out and only knew how to complain and regret making the wrong choice. I started to think that abandoning my executive career was a terrible idea and felt crazy about it. Had I really made the wrong decision?

Have you been through this, too? Watching everything in front of you fall apart, all while asking yourself what you are doing with your life?

Who She Think She Is?
Vivi Duarte

I saw those around me looking at me and asking about my choices as if starting a business was the worst decision. It was too heavy. I had two ways out, which is crucial for you to know. When you become an entrepreneur, you don't need to blame yourself if it doesn't work out, or if you discover in the middle of an avalanche, that it's not a fit for you. You can always go back and recalculate the route.

I didn't want to do this to myself, so I needed to act. My intuition told me not to give up. But it's okay if you think that's the best decision. After all, as they say, "no EIN is worth a stroke," and we know our limits.

It is essential to understand boundaries and mental health, and based on circumstances, make the best choice so that your body is not sacrificed. I was at my limit but decided I still had some energy left. I needed to get out of the fetal position and stop hiding in the face of debts and the nebulous situation I was facing in my business. I took a deep breath and reinspired myself with my story and the story of the women in my family. They fought so hard for me to be there and challenged by a business model neither of them had tried before. I was already a well-known journalist and occupied a place of privilege, even though I was in debt. You realize the importance of building your reputation and personal brand at these times. As my grandmother said, our name is all we have, and what we need to be The Woman we want to be, so we must always take care of it.

Who She Think She Is?

Vivi Duarte

I was breaking down and needed to act. No one was going to do this for me. Entrepreneurship has many solitary moments, as I already said. There are things that no one will do for you, no matter how much they love and admire you. There are things that only you can do for yourself, and I understood this and needed to save myself, my plans, and my company. I gathered my broken pieces from all the turbulent situations and tried to put together my plan as best I could. I went back to building an even more powerful network of partners and decided to move back to São Paulo–the city where everything happens. My hometown had been far away for years.

When I set up my business, I lived in Maringá, Paraná. It had around 400 thousand inhabitants who worked in commerce and agribusiness. There were a few multinational companies, and they all had different focuses from the clients I was looking for. Despite opening up many opportunities, the city had become too small for my plans, and I needed to do something about that.

I had a 12-year-old son and a stable life despite the troubles. I would flip everything upside down with my decision to return to São Paulo! So, I did! Because many times, that's exactly what we need to do. We have to act, and that's it. My son stayed with his father, who at the time was my husband and always supported me in my plans. And I came to São Paulo.

I stayed at my mother and sister's house for a while, but I soon realized that it is difficult to return and get used to a routine that is not ours once we leave our parent's home. I attended many events in my area to meet people and create a network of trust, which meant my schedule and lifestyle didn't fit into their household routine. I decided to look for a room in a small hotel that I could afford. I knew it could be dangerous, but I went to talk to the hotel staff who seemed very hospitable to me. I trusted that decision and soon made friends with everyone. They cared for me and my clothes, and the maid even ironed them and tidied up my room with all the care. It was a hot cubicle with a fan that only worked when it wanted to and made an unbearable noise. There was a small wardrobe, a single bed, and a fridge that didn't cool things properly, but it was what I had and could pay for. It was in a well-located neighborhood close to advertising agencies and important companies. I could attend meetings and events with peace of mind.

Do you see the scene? I was in a company where I was an executive in a cool position, and I made the decision to go into entrepreneurship. I turned everything upside down and decided that to gain traction and make my business happen, I would need to put myself out there without reservations and bet everything. As you read this, it may seem like an easy decision, but it wasn't. It never is. Giving up your comfort zone and privileges, no matter how minimal, is always painful. Sometimes, I looked at myself in the moldy mirror in my little room and cried. I'd look at the exhausted image of myself in the mirror and ask, "What am I doing here?"

I missed my son, who I saw every twenty days, and I missed having a good monthly salary in my account, health insurance, food vouchers, scheduled trips, and paid cards. My decision directly affected our family's financial health, and everyone suffered as a result. But I don't even know how to explain it. It pays off when you have a passion and purpose and believe in what you are doing. Take that calculated risk and get your foot in the door! I was there, standing at the door of the advertising market behind my opportunity. I was scared, but at the same time, I felt brave and confident.

Every day, I knocked on the doors of companies until I had the opportunity to present a special project to one of the largest advertising agencies in Brazil. I managed to schedule a meeting with the CEO of this agency, F.biz, which is part of the WPP group, Roberto Grosman, better known as Bob. I was so nervous that I entered the agency that day, tripping and toppling over a man. There was a lot of adrenaline, I needed to close a project, and this was a great opportunity. I knocked a person to the ground but not the project. He heard me out, even though he was stunned by the chaos of my disastrous arrival.

I presented an idea for one of the leading brands they serviced, Unilever's *Seda* shampoo. Bob called his team to watch my presentation and listen to my ideas. I was shaking, but I kept my cool. No one there could know I was broken. If there's one thing you need to learn in the world of business is to maintain emotional control and calmness, so at the moment of closing a deal, you don't desperately scream, "Let's close this, please! Give me this job. I need it! Trust me. You can pay in installments, and we can set up an exchange. Help me!". Never do that! Maintaining control is essential because any sign of weakness counts as negative points when you're starting.

In front of several executives from the agency, I presented the project which consisted of telling authentic stories of real women (outside the norm), giving protagonism, and a voice to them, and showing that there is beauty in diversity. Everyone loved it! Bob asked me to create proposals for two brands, one for the soap *Brilhante* and the other for hair with *Seda, using my idea*. And so, I closed my first million-dollar projects. "Beauty Hunters" with *Seda* and "*Brilliant Women*" with *Brilhante* powder detergent. Both projects gave protagonism to women in different ways and were the turning point in my journey.

In the in-between, I formed disastrous partnerships, but nothing that got in the way. I decided to dedicate hours of my day to working as a business consultant, and I soon managed to work for a multinational public relations company. It expanded my network of contacts in the market and increased the revenue for *Plano Feminino*. My plans seemed to finally be coming true. I did this for three years, learned a lot, and expanded my contact network with brands and agencies.

ALONE AND WELL-ACCOMPANIED

All my last slip-ups happened because I was totally stuck on the notion that I always needed someone by my side telling me what to do or validating my ideas to get them off the ground. I was used to this scenario without even realizing it. What would my mother and grandmother say about this?

I turned my energy and my thoughts to my childhood. To the muddy hills that I climbed with plastic bags on my feet. To all the insults that I, a girl born without privileges in a society that's based on standards, had to face. By remembering all this, I realized I had a lot of resilience and strength to accomplish anything I wanted. Having someone come in as a partner was just one detail, and I needed a more significant personal brand plan. Everyone should know me and my Plan.

CHAPTER 13

Kicked Out Of Church. Check!

I was always an energetic child who loved to attract attention. I constantly used my hairbrush as a microphone and interviewed my family and classmates. In school, I always tried to be a speaker or host of festivals. I loved theater and wrote plays based on the stories of comedians Chaves and Chapolin to act out with my friends from the street. They were the actors in the play that I directed and always starred in, of course. I wouldn't put in all that work and not act in it, right?

This passion pushed me to take some courses, and in my youth within the church, I became the leader of the Theatre Ministry. I led a group of young adults at an evangelical church that had very loud and lively worship bands and a short pastor who loved to impose his sexism in the form of preaching. I was in love with the Theater Ministry and the idea of bringing messages of love and liberation to people through huge performances for over two thousand people. It was like I had found my place in the world. I wrote, acted, communicated, and still felt connected with God by being inside his house and doing what was right. My mother always warned me not to stop studying, and I remained focused on my studies in college, but being in that theater ministry was important to me.

With all the knowledge I gained from the theater, I ended up teaching seniors at *Sesc* (Commerce Social Services) which was incredible. Through workshops I created for them,

80-year-olds were discovering themselves and their powers and bodies.

But, I had a big bump in the road. Despite being a great leader and speaker, that short pastor I mentioned was known in the church as a dictator and oppressive man. Sometimes, while we were singing in worship, he'd make many non-angelic expressions saying we were out of tune and disturbing him. I wondered if he was a perfectionist or if what he preached was incompatible with his actions. His attitude did not match the words said on the pulpit. That bothered me. One day, he decided they should remove me from the worship because I was too out of tune. Because I always questioned the sexism I saw in the church, he wanted to push me away. He ended up finding a way to expel me from the church. When I started working in a multinational company where I was forced to go on trips, and I could no longer dedicate myself as much as before, he discarded me once and for all. First, he said he didn't see a future in my career, repeating everything that I was already calloused from hearing: "I don't see a future for you in journalism, my daughter." "You question too much, and faith isn't something to be questioned." "Women need to put themselves in their place."

I fought back, didn't give up on my plans, and was expelled anyway. My entire network of trust, friends, and everything I held close, besides my family, was inside that church. I understood that a cycle was ending. I couldn't agree with the tyrannies of that pastor or the way he treated the people of the church. Everything about him irritated me. The tone of his voice, his demonic expressions for those singing out of tune, his sarcasm towards those who dared to demonstrate an opposite opinion, and the lack of female protagonists in that space. It was as if everyone lived to please him, not Christ. I didn't fit into that environment anymore. And even if I wanted to try, I had been expelled. My God, I was kicked out of church.

Have you ever been asked to leave a place you loved but knew it was time to go? Sometimes, it's a job you've been at for years where you know very well that you are stagnant and need to do something, but you don't have the courage. It could also be a relationship that is suffocating, but you got so used to sharing everything with that person that, even though they are weighing on your chest, you don't have the courage to remove them. You know how it works, and it happens to everyone. And on those occasions, you become sad and melancholic, maybe out of ego or out of sheer tantrums, thinking that it wasn't you who made the decision to leave. But the fact is after the emptiness comes the feeling of freedom and the possibility of something new that invades your life and makes you wake up feeling light again. You wake up, and the page has turned and is waiting for you to write another chapter. Have you ever felt this? Are you going through this now? Is it time to turn the page? How long will you wait to change your story? Will you wait until you're expelled, or will you get out of there?

I'm telling you all this because, in the next chapter, we'll talk about building our personal brand. We are often not proud of our stories. And we end up not valuing things you consider unimportant, although they are. Amidst the glamorization of life exposed on Instagram, Facebook, and LinkedIn, you might devalue important moments. On Instagram, everyone travels and frequents incredible places. On Facebook, everyone has the best opinions. On LinkedIn, everyone is successful. On social media, no one has ever failed to pay a bill or keep their payroll up-to-date. Nobody ever had to count their miles to purchase a vacation package or beg for a job opening because they couldn't survive another month without work. There are so many perfect lives that, if we compare them to ours, we end up thinking we're a failed project.

Then you ask yourself, "How can my story be interesting compared to all these successful people?" "Wow, my life is so boring. Everyone else's is much more interesting." "My image is not that cool. I don't know how I could sell my company and business from such a normal person like me..." Do you recognize yourself in any of these phrases? Well, that has to change!

Who She Think She Is?

Vivi Duarte

CHAPTER 14

Your Story Has Value –

Build Your Brand

Who She Think She Is?

Vivi Duarte

I always hear my students talking about themselves from this perspective. Do you know what I tell them? Building your brand starts with valuing yourself, your stories, and your experiences, even if your biography includes being kicked out of a church or tying plastic bags on your feet to get to and from school.

Your story has value. These difficult situations are an important lesson, and they will provide you with a thick skin to help you become The Woman you want to be.

It's worth believing in who you are and valuing your story without comparing yourself to anyone. The worst thing you can do is compare your life to others and value other people's stories more than yours. Each of us has a different starting point which makes all the difference in our journey. Being inspired is one thing. Wanting to be another person or belittling yourself because you think they have a better and more interesting life than yours is like shooting yourself in the foot. Never do that. Never hide yourself. Because I was invalidated by people I considered spiritual leaders, I could have thought that I was a terrible person and a useless communicator. But when you're around critics who try to show you your faults, focus on your strengths and qualities instead.

Look in the mirror, talk to yourself, and remind yourself of your dreams, only taking with you constructive criticism. Throw away everything else.

To build your personal brand, you will need to work on your self-esteem. This involves respecting your story and understanding that each little piece of you is preparing you to be The Woman of your dreams. Be proud of this and use your experiences to your advantage.

BE A SHOWOFF

We always hear that it's better to not show off too much. In journalism, for example, I learned that I had to be impartial and that the news was always the protagonist. So, I couldn't think about showing off. Even if you are the anchor, you will only be the channel for the story but it will still be the main subject. Maybe that's why I always stayed behind the scenes and never went on stage. When I launched my business, I had never worked on my image. People didn't associate my image with the *Plano Feminino* and that was something I needed to improve. I needed to put my face in the sun and build my personal brand.

I had been doing this for many years by helping executives position themselves in the market. But I got too comfortable. I then decided that everyone should know more about me, my business, and my purpose.

YOUR IMAGE

Before you build your image to others, it needs to be aligned with your essence and make sense to you. You can't wear clothes that are uncomfortable or not made for your measurements. You need to revisit the past, pay attention to the present, and picture the future.

Who are you so far?

What are you doing right now?

Where do you want to go?

Answering these questions gave me direction and helped me find exactly where I wanted to go. I revisited my whole life, and my stance on each point of contact. I asked my closest friends and colleagues what they saw in me and what strengths and weaknesses I had demonstrated with my actions.

I discovered that people believed in me and saw me as a strong and inspiring woman. Deep down, without modesty, I knew that I was this woman. I never stopped believing, but this exercise was necessary for me to see myself as complete and to take the stage with my plan. I was the face and no one else.

I started designing each touchpoint of my personal brand. When we create a marketing strategy for a brand or product we come up with its essence, persona, values, mission, and vision. We map out each point of contact where this brand can interact to plan their actions strategically so that they acquire reputation and relevance. I did this with orange juice, makeup, health insurance, etc. However, I had never done it for myself. That's what I would do from that moment on. I invite you to do the same as I explain each point. I will help you design an action plan.

Mission

The mission is our reason for existing and can change when we achieve what we want. It can be recalculated along the way based on lessons learned. I like the story of Mary Kay, a female entrepreneur who managed to form a network of female accomplices for her plans. Her company's mission was to give unlimited opportunities to women.

Looking internally, what is your mission in this world?

Through this exercise, I discovered that my mission was much more than to change the narrative of Brazilian advertising and redefine its stereotypes. My mission was to inspire girls and women to achieve their plans. Discovering this changed everything within me and my business.

Values

Values are everything that we do not negotiate, exchange, or bargain. Have you ever thought about what yours are? Sometimes we don't even know our values and we end up getting into toxic relationships, abusive friendships, and circles of people who have nothing to do with us, allowing others to live our lives for us.

When revisiting my values, I realized that I had overlooked a lot of important things. In recent years, I was allowing people with much less career experience than me to give their opinions on my work and put me down. I heard destructive criticism from those who had never done half as much as I had in life, yet I took it into consideration. Then I realized I needed to get these people out of my life. I removed people who infiltrated my life that needed to go. Additionally, I served clients and brands that had nothing to do with my essence, and felt like a fraud.

To design my new values, I made a list of negotiables and non-negotiables. Everything I could be flexible with and everything I never wanted near me, personally and professionally.

NEGOTIABLE	NON-NEGOTIABLE
Changing the route of my plans	Toxic people that put me down
Listening to opposing opinions, but only ones that have backing	Feeling like a fraud
Delegate tasks	Wanting to do everything alone

Vision

My mission is what I do, my values are who I am, and my vision is what I want to achieve.

My mission is what I do.
My values are who I am, and my
vision is what I want to achieve.
My mission is what I do, my
values are who I am, and my
vision is what I want to achieve.
My mission is what I do, my
values are who I am, and my
vision is what I want to achieve.
My mission is what I do, my
values are who I am, and my
vision is what I want to achieve.
My mission is what I do, my
values are who I am, and my
vision is what I want to achieve.
My mission is what I do, my
values are who I am, and my
vision is what I want to achieve.

Your vision is the dream you want to achieve. It's when you look at your future without reservations and limitations, expand your field of vision to all you can accomplish. Do this for yourself. Clear the limiting factors from your mind and dare to dream of The Woman you want to become. Where will she be? How? Doing what? Having a vision of your world changes everything and helps you make choices in the present that will get you there.

Learn the following:

"A *brand* is the story that consumers remember when they think of a business, and it's not just a design or marketing task, but the responsibility of everyone within a company; essentially highlighting that branding is an active process, not just a static logo image."
- **Laura Busche**, author of *Lean Branding. Creating Dynamic Brands to Generate Conversion.*

"When people use your brand name as a verb, that is remarkable."
- **Meg Whitman**, one of the most powerful executives in the world

I mapped out all my points of contact, just like I did in strategies for brands. So, I started to devise a plan on how to position myself in the best way for each of these points. I'll share with you the questions I asked myself and what I did to change. I encourage you to do this reflection exercise as well.

Facebook

Who are you in your timeline? Do the things you share align with your vision, your mission, and your values? Which emoticons do you provoke with your posts? Do you add value or cause discord? How do you share your powers on Facebook? How do people understand who you are and what you are doing?

LinkedIn

What does your profile photo look like and what have you shared through it? Have you created an interesting network of connections? How do you interact with them? Have you been posting relevant comments?

Instagram

We know real life is not an organized feed with a planned-out color palette. Don't fool yourself, and don't compare yourself! Social media is capable of causing psychological problems, as the virtual environment is a favorable space for people to compare themselves and believe in what is just a slice of reality. The insane search for likes and followers has significantly impacted people's self-esteem. Even Instagram itself has been rethinking the issue of viewing likes.

WhatsApp & Messaging Apps

Pay attention to the group chats you join. This will make a big difference in your life.

Why are you in group chats that only make you lose focus? Why do you intend to use this communication channel? Whom is it you want to connect through it?

I realized that I wasted a lot of time responding to messages that weren't a priority and how counterproductive this was. It took the focus away from things that mattered, leaving me more exhausted and with a headache. So, I decided to mute some group chats, ask for permission, or simply leave some. I started not responding to messages so quickly. Many times, it was people who came to me so I could solve their problems. I needed to organize the avalanche of messages and contacts I connected with daily. Organizing this mess made me focus on what really mattered.

Events

I asked myself what the most important events I would need to attend to meet people. So, I mapped out the main ones and contacted the organizers. I made myself available to speak and cover the content. I offered my best, and this exchange made me get on the radar of the main events that interested me. I met people with the same purposes as mine at different stages of their journeys making me learn and inspired me to continue.

Personal Life

After almost five years as an entrepreneur, I had no personal life anymore.

There is a photo circulating on the internet where several characters are sleeping: a student, an intern, an executive, and, instead of an entrepreneur, the bed appears empty. It seems funny, but this message is the cruel truth. Most of the time, being an entrepreneur makes us lose sleep or work 48 hour days. When we realize it, we no longer have a social life or friends. And family, when you're lucky, are the only ones who will always be there following you and waiting for crumbs of attention.

I realized I needed to pay more attention to the people I loved because connecting to them recharged me. They gave me the energy to follow through on my plans.

Work

I began to control my impulse to create new things better and dedicate myself to running the products of my consulting company. I started remodeling and sophisticating deliveries and developing a strategic flowchart so my team could have more autonomy in decision-making.

I understood that I didn't know how to delegate tasks, and I was a controlling manager. That is, I didn't allow people to learn and acquire self-confidence to perform tasks without my approval. I wanted to be present throughout the entire process, all the time, and it was exhausting. I hired trustworthy people and started delegating more and focusing on strategies and long-term ideas. Changing my management vision and delegating more allowed me to have time to write this book. To give you an idea of how much has changed, when I took a few days to finish this book, my team was at the office hosting a major event for one of our main clients, defining content strategies, and operating an expansion plan.

When you are an entrepreneur or intrapreneur, you want to give more than 100% in business. You believe that isolating all other areas of your life to carry out a plan is the best thing you can do, but that is not true. When you learn to look strategically at each point of
contact in your life and create an improvement action plan for each area, you understand that one complements the other. You will only be complete when you understand this.

Time for yourself

One day in between meetings, I bent down to pick up a pen that had fallen under the table when I heard a noise. I felt the cold of the air conditioning on my back and realized that I had torn a shirt that loved. I thought my new dryer had shrunk my clothes, so I continued working. The next day, I noticed that my pants were frayed, and I felt cramped inside them. At the end of the day when I took them off, there were marks on my legs from the tight jeans. I found it strange, but another piece of clothing was lost because of the dryer. Maybe I had gained some pounds with my frenetic routine? Could it be the frozen foods and tubs of ice cream that I consumed late at night while watching TV to take my mind off hard days at work? I went to the bathroom and pulled out the scale under the closet to weigh myself (something I hadn't done in a long time). Bingo. I had gained twenty-six pounds and hadn't even realized it!

Who She Think She Is?

Vivi Duarte

As a teenager, I suffered from anorexia when I was struggling to have the body of the skinny girls on magazine covers. They were all white and had completely different hip and bust measurements from me. I got to the point where I stopped menstruating, and I needed medical treatment to return to a healthy life. The lack of representation in advertising has always affected me. Certainly, this was one of the reasons I fought against this after graduating in communication and marketing. Media and advertising vehicles need to understand they are responsible for their narratives and that the reflection of the invisibility of colors and bodies that they promote can kill.

Because of my anorexia, I hardly weigh myself. I try to take care of my diet and maintain an balanced lifestyle with exercise. But who said being an entrepreneur would allow me the time to take care of myself? It had been months since I'd spent time with myself, gone to pilates, went for a walk, or even looked closely at what I was eating. I was living on autopilot and in the self-destructive mode of working as hard as you can imagine. I looked at the scale, and all I could think about was how I was self-sabotaging. How many triggers could be activated from that information? A person who has an eating disorder always has to take care of their mind so they don't return to the dark place of looking in the mirror and invalidating themselves. I was happy with my image but feeling tired and fatigued. The answer was in those twenty-six extra pounds.

So, I decided to enroll in a swimming class at a gym and do the things I loved: swimming and training for races. Without a lot of pressure, I started training once or twice a week and started looking more carefully at my diet and my hours of sleep. Little by little, I'm getting along better. However, I need discipline and self-care, so I don't let anything stop me from having time for myself. Sometimes it seems like everything is more important than having time to dedicate to yourself, but it's not! One of the best investments is being in your own company and enjoying it, while doing something you love without pressure just because you really want to do it.

Society

When I started designing my personal brand and rebuilding my identity with my mission, vision, values , and passions, I found in myself what has always motivated me: my interpersonal relationships superpower and the way I like to see people around me happy. Sometimes I sabotaged myself and, to make people happy, neglected my desires. But, in general, that was what I knew to do best, and everything was always thought about in collectives, groups, and circles. I've always been good at selling ideas, and my ideas were always related to collective change and transformation. Proof of this is that my business model is a consultancy that, since 2010, has challenged large advertising agencies to part ways with standards and

139

stereotypes, including black, fat, tall, or short people in their campaigns, thus creating a new narrative with more empowerment, representation, and diversity. It was never just about one product. When I reflected on that, I returned to the girl I was.

Even though I was in the middle of the entrepreneurial chaos while trying to reposition and give voice to my image and the business, I was now a privileged woman. I would need to do something with my privileges.

What are you going to do with the privileges you have in your hands?

That's the question I asked myself, and you must ask when you pass this pillar to think about building your personal brand.

People have increasingly turned to their essence and sought their purpose, even though we compare ourselves so much on social media and are inserted in a world desperate for results. With so many demands from the capitalist world, in which human beings seem to have less value than the things, people feel diminished. Having appears to be more important than being. That is, values seem to be subverted, and that is why the existential void only increases and nothing fills it (even if you achieve material goods). Something's missing. We have a lack of purpose. In this search for real meaning, many gurus emerged and took the opportunity to charge elevated amounts to simply tell their customers something that no one but themselves could discover: their purpose and their essence. All you have to do is go back to the basics whenever you feel lost and diminished in this crazy world.

Some brands have been talking about this. I help some find a greater purpose than just selling their products, to impact consumers' lives genuinely and sincerely. But how can we as individuals do this too? I started to ask myself this and returned to my essence. The essence of a girl who was born on the outskirts of São Paulo, and all she had was her mother's and grandmother's mentorship. They were the only ones who believed I could be what I wanted to be, even though other people discredited me and laughed at me because they saw me as a statistic.

As I remembered the girl I was and The Woman I had become, I decided I had to do something with the privilege I gained of being in a different social place than I experienced. That's why I decided to create a social project to tell girls from the outskirts that it was possible to dream, have plans, and make them come true. I created *Plano de Menina*, a project to connect my entire network of contacts through workshops, from powerful women to girls from small communities. Judges, prosecutors, advertisers, businesswomen, entrepreneurs, doctors, journalists, economists, administrators, psychologists, lawyers. Women from different areas of expertise joined me to help outskirt girls become protagonists of their stories.

In this project, they take classes in financial education, entrepreneurship, self-esteem, law, toxic relationships, programming, social media, brand persona, and others that make them break the bubble and recognize themselves as powerful. Once they graduate, we connect these girls to young apprentice positions within partner companies.

Creating this social mission saved me, rescued my vision, and showed what I was really doing here. In 2019, the *Plano de Menina* began to have a methodology replicated in other states in Brazil and is becoming an institute. Since 2016, more than two thousand girls have gone through the program and had their lives and those of their families transformed for the better. This is, without a doubt, the best plan I've ever had in my whole life. I want to live each day to dedicate myself more and more to it.

After mapping out how to share your world with your main points of contact, it's time to put each plan into action. To do this, you must put yourself first and learn to negotiate and choose your battles.

BE PROUD OF YOUR STORY TRANSFORM
EVERYTHING INTO LESSONS AND LEGACY

Plano de Menina, one of the most respected institutes in the country, wasn't born from commissioned research, from no opportunistic feeling, and not "surfing the wave of purpose." It was born from within me on June 3rd, 1978.

It was born from the experience of a dreamer who had the obstacles of every girl born without privileges in Brazil. A girl who dreamed of being a journalist and heard, "College is not for poor people."

I felt the self-centered assistance of privileged people from international NGOs who circulated the outskirts to investigate how "those people" lived and what they ate. They thought "those people" needed donations, not intellectual and economic empowerment. Why do poor people need to go to college, right?

But the girl I was didn't want just food. I wanted more. Here I am, building something I hoped for as a child and never had. A project that saw me as powerful and not maintenance. Here I am. The woman who once was a girl who had to chase after everything that was denied. Who went through so much sleep deprivation to be able to study and prove that she deserved to occupy the space she wanted, building a bridge of access to outskirt girls with the privileges I achieved.

I'm building a bridge so that the girls in this project have the opportunity to recognize, sooner than I did, their power and

143

to prepare themselves to take up space with their heads held high, without ever forgetting their origin and the power of TOGETHER, gratitude, and the network that we are building every year.

No one does anything alone and honoring every opportunity by doing our best for all is what makes us stronger. There are many of us and we are spreading throughout Brazil. This will be the stage they will be on soon to share their big plans with the world. Another space we will occupy TOGETHER.

Plano de Menina was born from a woman who experienced firsthand what it means to be a female Brazilian dreamer without privileges and is strong and ready to occupy and open spaces so that all the girls who are still in this condition have a voice and a place and be protagonists of their stories!

What can you do to build a better society? How can you become an agent of transformation with what you have available to you? *Plano de Menina* started without investment, with only the best of resources a person can have; a defined purpose and network of accomplices.

Amid the COVID-19 pandemic, we managed to train and employ hundreds of girls in large companies. In 2019, we carried out our festival at the largest museum in Latin America, MASP (The São Paulo Art Museum), with thousands of people. Do you see how having a purpose helps us go further?

What is your network and your purpose?

TURN UP THE VOLUME

My first experience as a leader in a company left me quite introspective about what was wrong with me or whether there even was something wrong!

I was always prepared for meetings, but I couldn't speak a word. I was the only woman in the room, and the men competed on who was the loudest and had the best idea. I thought that interrupting those know-it-all men was impractical, and I went unnoticed in meetings for months.

Sometimes, they asked me to write down what they said, and I'd become the scribe at my peers' meetings. I knew this wasn't right, but I didn't know how to take a stand.

We once received a survey from a giant multinational company on Brazilian consumption behavior. I read all the material, wrote down my inputs and ideas, and prepared for the research meeting. Something held me back in meetings, and I just didn't understand if it was shyness or simply the cruel force of patriarchy. But that day, I can't say what it was. I had been possessed by self-esteem and a spirit of justice for myself, which was stronger than my insecurity. When the meeting began, the men started the dispute of egos once again. However, I realized that none of those there had prepared or read that research more than me. It was my chance to take my place. So, I started talking over them. They ignored and talked over me while repeating what I had just said. That's when I raised my voice and said, "Please! Let me speak! You are repeating exactly what I'm saying. Bring new facts or let me finish. Please." They all stopped while looking at each other, somewhat stunned by my firmness, so I continued. I explained that I had read all the research and made a report with the main themes of interest for the product launch. I brought my experience to the table, which was surrounded by deafening silence. I could have apologized at the moment. After all, that's what we learn to do as women: apologize or blame ourselves for things that have nothing to do with us. But I preferred not to and concluded my thought. When I finished, the first thing I heard from my superior was whether I was ok or if there was a problem!

He wanted to tell me that I shouldn't have interrupted just to give my opinion, and my behavior had been inconvenient (despite the sexist bunch not giving me an opportunity). I said yes, that I was doing great, and that I would like to know my colleague's views on the information I had shared. Everyone expressed their opinions and respected my speaking time, and from then on, I started to understand the game. I was no longer going to remain silent. I wouldn't self-sabotage anymore. If they didn't give me space to speak, I would conquer it myself.

There's no point in creating a brand persona, mapping points of contact, changing social media profile photos, or creating support and interest networks if all you do is remain silent and let others speak for you when the time comes to act. Being the protagonist of your story will depend on your attitude in the face of different situations, and one of them is not allowing yourself to be interrupted or sabotaged. Never think your idea is not the best and that it shouldn't be discussed even if you're not ready to enter the game. Get ready and use the weapons you have. Information and technique combined with self-confidence are the tools that, if exercised daily, will help build your brand in the business world.

You will need to pick your battles. You can't be reactive in every meeting you attend. Some things are better left undiscussed and let go, as I did in a particular situation. I was in a meeting with two female executives, and they constantly interrupted each other. It was a pathetic scene of a power struggle that only demonstrated the lack of union between women. Unfortunately, this is a reality that happens all the time, no matter how much we fight against it. It became evident that the two were competing for their own space in the company. I was a supplier, and I often wanted to ask them to listen to each other and pay attention to what was happening in that meeting. However, I understood that I wasn't the one who could change that scenario, so I should have simply done my job and ended the meeting. Choosing your battles will preserve your mental health and your energy to focus on what really matters. Choose yours wisely.

LEARN TO SELL YOUR IDEAS

I grew up in a household of saleswomen who were not ashamed to go out onto the streets and sell their products. Ultimately, they had a greater purpose: putting food on the table.

Understanding that you must become a salesperson to achieve your goals is essential to eliminate any prejudice.

All my experiences as a salesperson for clothes, shoes, decor, and even telemarketing helped me become a good negotiator and seller of plans and ideas. People give this role different names because they seem ashamed to call themselves salespeople. After all, it doesn't sound fancy to be a saleswoman. But knowing how to sell is essential and will help you bring your big plans to life.

You can start developing your sales skills by removing this preconceived notion and asking yourself: Who better than myself to convince someone that my idea is good? That my product works? That my work has value? If you are sure of this, no one will stop you from selling your ideas.

Create a business plan in which you can visualize all the points of your idea/product and write everything down:

Who She Think She Is?
Vivi Duarte

What is your plan?

What is your objective?

What's it for?

How is it different?

Who's your target audience?

Who's your indirect audience?

Who are your direct competitors?

Who are your indirect competitors?

What are your strengths?

What are your weaknesses?

What are the threats?

What are the opportunities?

GODDESS PITCH

Write a defense for your plan here as if you were presenting your business to a major investor and had only five minutes. Be creative, you got this!

YOU FIRST

My career as an executive taught me that everything has limits and that almost cost me my mental health. You know that concept of a team? The whole all for one and one for all? I always fell for the "one for all and no one for one". Suddenly, I found myself doing several favors for my superiors, my peers, and even my interns. She was cute, sweet, and the savior of jobs. At first, this seemed incredible, but in reality, it was consuming me. Saying yes to everything and being afraid of being annoying by saying "I can't" was making me overwhelmed and very depressed. I did everything for everyone and was not recognized for any of it. And worse, all this demand for "yes" left me with no time to invest in my own career.

I had a colleague who always counted on me, but when I needed her, she could never help me. There was a colleague who didn't like doing spreadsheets and passed them on to me because I was very organized. There was a bit of everything. Have you ever been through this?

Who She Think She Is?
Vivi Duarte

Here are two things I discovered: learning to say no will help you gain respect and putting yourself first is not selfish, it is self-love.

When we understand this, it is liberating. Think about that announcement we hear before the plane takes off that says:

"In the event of decompression of the cabin, oxygen masks will fall automatically. Pull one of the masks, place it over your nose and mouth, adjust the elastic around the head, and breathe normally, then help the person next to you."

This is exactly what we need to do in life: put ourselves and our self-care first. And this applies to all areas of life.

I remember the first time I said "I can't do this for you" to a co-worker. At that moment in the face of judgment and her disbelief, I realized that it was no longer a favor, it was an obligation. I felt like retreating from her look of disappointment and judgment, but I remained firm in my purpose. I needed to stand up for myself and put myself above other people's demands. I needed to assume my protagonist in that space. And that was what I did.

To fill the only vacancies available, they created the idea that we must compete with each other and put each other down if we want our time in the sun. The worst thing is that we believe them, we separate ourselves, we hate each other, and we hunt each other to this day.

We can't love someone more than ourselves.
We can't help anyone more than ourselves.
We cannot dedicate ourselves to someone or
something more than we do to ourselves.
We can't let everyone get ahead while we leave
ourselves behind.

Sisterhood

Now I need to talk about a very important topic: sisterhood.

In the corporate world, we women are slowly learning about sisterhood. We still earn 30% less exercising the same roles as men. We are still passed over when we return from maternity leave since they place us in unknown areas and weaken our performance in the company. We are a tiny number on company councils. And, if we consider racial issues, Black women occupy 0.4% of a company's leadership positions. This hostile environment in corporations reflects the reality of a sexist, racist, and patriarchal society.

The concept of sisterhood arrived to "turn up the volume" on the importance of coming together to break down barriers and misogynistic standards. This hasn't been easy. Some women opt for selective sisterhood and only help those who are like them. Some women take advantage of the term to exploit other women. Not everything is chaos. We are moving forward in unity.

But what is sisterhood?

This word means a lot to us women: our unity, strength, and alliance together to deconstruct and redefine sexist and patriarchal concepts that greatly weaken us, making us believe that we need to be enemies and rivals towards each other. Sisterhood helps us have empathy with each other, avoiding

153

prior judgment, so that we can strengthen ourselves and occupy spaces in society with a common goal: gender equality and the fight for our rights.

The word "sisterhood" means powerful unity between women. We need to come together more and more, but truly and healthily. You can't say it's sisterhood when it's just you being there for another woman, and she can never support you in anything. Pay close attention to your relationships, and never forget that character is independent of gender. Build your network of women who support each other and respect your time and your choices. No is no in any situation.

If you are an entrepreneur, this also applies to business partnerships. Many people may ask to get coffee with you, and it becomes a free private consultant session. In other words, an enormous lack of elegance and empathy that would leave anyone in a delicate situation. Some people ask for free services, plagiarize your ideas, or want to form partnerships that demand a lot from you and offer very little in return. If everyone around you is smiling while sucking your energy without offering anything meaningful in return, put an end to it immediately. Say no. Review your partners. Set boundaries. Be objective and transparent. Don't be afraid to say no.

Here are some tips:

1. Make it clear what partnership is for you: an exchange.

2. Make time for coffee dates with people who are interesting, share ideas, and bring value to you and your business.

3. Establish specific pro bono services in your business and communicate this when your presence is requested for free at any place.

4. Make it clear what is unacceptable to you and, clearly and objectively, say what interests you.

5. Use "no" to your advantage and without fear. If you know what you don't want, you already have 50% of your plan accomplished.

Finally, let go of the victim role and take control of your life!

Never negotiate your essence.

Never negotiate your essence.

Never negotiate your essence.

Never negotiate your essence.

Never negotiate your essence.

Never negotiate your essence.

Never negotiate your essence.

Never negotiate your essence.

Never negotiate your essence.

Never negotiate your essence.

Never negotiate your essence.

Never negotiate your essence.

Never negotiate your essence.

Never negotiate your essence.

Who She Think She Is?

Vivi Duarte

CHAPTER 15

Who Are You Amid Chaos?

Who She Think She Is?

Vivi Duarte

I need to share with you that writing this book took about two years. Today I am 46 and will soon be 47. It took me a while to complete because I felt insecure, and I self-sabotaged for months. I deleted everything I wrote and started again. Throughout this process and in every word I wrote, I found myself again. I was moved when I realized that every moment of my life, the good and especially the bad, contributed to me becoming The Woman I always dreamed of being. I also realized that each decision made a difference and that honoring The Woman I idealized for my future was also important. I need to thank little Vivi who never gave up and who, amidst the chaos, stood firmly with her head held high and chased her dreams so that I could live the life I am living today. That's why I insist on telling you to honor each experience along the way and make choices that honor The Woman you are and who you want to be one day.

While writing this book, I became a grandmother to a beautiful girl named Luiza. The daughter of my 21-year-old only son, Paulo.

My son has become an incredible guy. He graduated in marketing and today works at one of the most renowned banks in the country. He's won, for the second consecutive year, recognition as the company's employee of excellence. I'm very proud of him, and my heart overflows when I remember that we'd go to my college classes together as he'd sit quietly waiting for me to finish. We faced a lot of chaos together. But it was important for him to learn resilience. All of this helps in all areas of his life!

Luiza, my granddaughter, is my four-leaf clover and encouraged me to make big decisions in my life. She inspired me to show her that we can accommodate ourselves and be satisfied with crumbs of anything. We must honor the women we are and the women we want to become. She is full of herself and her nickname is Miss Mini Jaguar, since mine is Miss Jaguar. Despite being young, she already knows very well what she wants, and if someone gets in her way and takes it away, she rebels. It's great being a grandmother and being able to see Luiza grow up and achieve her plans.

While writing this book, I completed an important and lesson-filled cycle: a 25-year marriage. I want to thank my ex-partner, father of my son and grandfather of my granddaughter, for the entire journey here, and wishing you so much happiness.

I got into dating apps to understand how relationships work at the moment, and I met some crazy people and some cool people. I'm relearning and learning a lot in this area.

During the preparation of this book, something unprecedented happened in the world: the COVID-19 pandemic. The year 2020 became the most confusing, disturbing and transformative for us all. The moment I wrote this book while in Brazil, there have been more than 200 thousand deaths. The second country with the most deaths in the world because of an insane, perverse, and sadistic government that oppresses minorities and ignores the virus.

What can we do? How should we behave in the midst of this pandemic? It's time to ask yourself: Who are you in the midst of chaos? The Woman that solves the problem? The one that creates more problems? The one who hides? The one who ignores the problems? The one who goes into despair?

It is important for us to know who we are especially in chaotic moments. Ask yourself. Notice yourself.

Understand who your allies are in difficult times and never forget it. It is important to have your circle of trust and work on your resistance to get through difficult times and maintain an unshakeable mental health.

During the pandemic, I had to review many *Plano Feminino* and *Instituto Plano de Menina* products and services. We transformed in-person lectures into online experiences, created educational journeys via video calls, held dozens of live streams with incredible women, employed girls in global companies, and built projects with brands that generated great results. I had to look at the chaos and not give in. I had to establish plans that could sustain me, not discourage me. I needed to take care of myself, and sometimes, cry quietly with the uncertainty so as not to demotivate my team. But the next day, I was ready to start everything over again.

I also understood that vulnerability is vital, so we can build ourselves into strong women. Stereotypes that we aren't allowed to show fear of and insecurity can drive us crazy. I started sharing my fears with my team and my closest friends, and it worked. No one is an island and sometimes you need to break down to rebuild your plans.

While writing this book, I also accepted a new professional challenge. I decided to diversify my business, something I had been craving for a while. I took on the position of CEO of Buzzfeed Brazil in October 2020. Buzzfeed is the third most accessed content platform in Brazil, and it speaks to a generation that interests me a lot: millennials. The internet has been too polarized. Content needs to attract young people to information in a faster and more interesting way. The objective is to consistently be the most relevant news and entertainment decoder for this audience. I'm excited for all my plans to come to fruition and for us to redefine the internet with purposeful content and great projects for brands where everyone wins. Business with purpose is the key for you to differentiate yourself, and I'm focused on that.

I heard many people questioning what I was doing by occupying another CEO chair. Do you know what I answered? That sometimes people won't understand you, and that's their problem. So, follow your path and believe in yourself!

I remembered Angela Davis's emblematic and powerful phrase that says: "When a Black woman moves, the whole structure of society moves with her." I feel that way. Amidst the chaos, I blossomed from the inside out. I was exhausted from the quarantine, no creativity, and a desire to cry. But there's something that made all the difference: I didn't back down!

Who She Think She Is?
Vivi Duarte

How many of us endured it? Many of us stopped and left our dreams behind. Our head hurts and we feel fear taking over our bodies and paralyzing us. We prefer to let go of our dreams and just get on with our lives. If you're doing this to take care of your mental health, then yes, take care of yourself. However, find a way to resume your plans. Don't give up on yourself. Don't give up on The Woman who you dreamed and dared to want to become before you knew there would be obstacles, lack of privileges, betrayals, and other negative aspects. Believe in yourself and carry on with your plans. Create your network of allies, go to therapy, find your support to conquer what is yours.

When we discover who we are and learn to move through chaos and survive, we understand that we can be whatever we want. Some of us will move forward quickly because we came from privileged space. Others, like you and me, will have to fight ten times more. But the important thing is that we won't stop. We won't give up on ourselves. When you reach the spaces you always dreamed of occupying: look to the side, bring other women up, and be a bridge. Do your part and let's take up our space of power in society together.

You can do this! I believe in you.

Go team!

CHAPTER 16

For All

TO YOU, BLACK WOMAN

I discovered I was black at age 37. Yes, mixed-race families and whitewashing do this to us. I am a black woman with passability by having facial features and hair palatable to the racist gaze of society. Of course, that's what made me think I was "just tan," as everyone around me said. However, when it came to promotions, competition, and opportunities, I always had to fight five or ten times harder. My obstacle wasn't just being born without privileges. I fought it, and the colorism privileges allowed me to hack this unequal system. But this doesn't happen to the majority of us. It's exhausting. It hurts. But I want you to know that you are not alone. We are together.

Today, occupying the chairs of privileges that I have conquered, I am building bridges so that you can also occupy your spaces. Not just me, but other black women are doing it. It's tiring, but don't give up on yourself and your goals. Promise yourself this and do your best. Rejoice in the small achievements of each day. They will support you in building what you want.

Be proud of The Woman you are and honor your ancestors. Be strategic and make alliances. We still earn less. There is still no equity in spaces of power, but we will be in greater numbers one day. Each one that arrives is valuable and represents us. Respect your story and go for it!

Use this space to write yourself a letter about always prioritizing yourself and never giving up on who you are:

_____

_____

_____

_____

_____

_____

_____

_____

_____

_____

_____

_____

_____

_____

_____

_____

_____

_____

TO YOU, WHITE WOMAN

Being born white in a racist country is a privilege, regardless of the region you're from. This already gives you the green light to move around and occupy your spaces. Of course, you will encounter obstacles. But no one will stop you or look at you suspiciously in a store because you are looking for your cell phone inside your bag.

You will likely reach your goals faster. Knowing your privilege as a white woman and the responsibility it comes with is very important.

Conquer all your plans.

Believe in yourself.

And when you get to the space you want to be in, bring along black women.

Be friends with black women.

Use your privileges to change this perverse game of structural racism. You have everything to do with this, and your choices will make a difference in building a society with more racial equity, in which everyone can have a voice and a chance to be The Woman they want to be.

Use this space to write yourself a letter answering the following question: What can I do today with my privileges?

_____

_____

_____

_____

_____

_____

_____

_____

_____

_____

_____

_____

_____

_____

_____

_____

_____

_____

_____

TO ALL

Use this space to write down everything you're proud of being and what you desire to build. Who do you want to be?

_____

_____

_____

_____

_____

_____

_____

_____

_____

_____

_____

_____

_____

_____

_____

_____

_____

_____

Bonus Content

Dictionary

Here, you will find expressions that I created to describe certain situations in everyday business life.

Cute crazy: In extreme situations, where you need to put a person in their place, act "cute" and use firm words. A soft tone of voice with sharp words will warp the head of anyone who is underestimating you. Show them who's in control and smile, you're being recorded, you cutie!

Completing the rainbow: When the situation doesn't concern you and you want to pretend that you didn't understand, that you didn't hear anything, or that you didn't see what was happening, look far away, maintain a calm appearance, and blend in. Go out to get a coffee and only come back when the weather is better. This works for personal relationships too.

Phony from the Nile: Some people are just great actors, right? They're always out of orbit. Some people pretend to be stupid and take advantage of the situation. In the business world, there are many phonies and one of them, in strategic moments, can be you. Stay alert in the game.

Victory in war: It is about choosing which battles you want to fight and which ones you will stick to till the end. Choose your battles for the sake of your mental health.

Those kinds of people: Stay away from people who always reach out to you for our contacts and are never available for anything.

Toxic friends: People who only criticize and bring you down don't need to be by your side.

Rocket Friends: Connect with people who celebrate your achievements and inspire you to fly even higher, supporting you along the way.

Reminders

Stick these on your forehead, the fridge, the closet, and the mirror!

1. Have a support network with people who have the same energy and desire to achieve as you: employees, suppliers, and partners.

2. Don't wait for perfection to put your projects out there. Things can be built along the way. Of course, only if your idea really has some value and purpose.

3. Prioritize time for the people you love and for yourself. It is love that fuels us to face everyday life!

4. Don't take on the role of superhero. Sometimes things go wrong, and that's okay. Work passionately and be honest with yourself and the people around you. You will certainly reap what you sow; always remember that!

5. Value your time. Sometimes that means not being able to get coffee with all the interesting people that come into your life or going to all the events that people invite you to.

6. Priority is everything in this life. Prioritize yourself and be ruthless about it.

7. Be resilient and keep believing in people.

8. Have the courage to be The Woman you want to be.

Who She Think She Is?
Vivi Duarte

About The Author

Vivi Duarte is the founder and CEO of PLANO, a consultancy founded 14 years ago to promote narratives in advertising and corporate initiatives, promoting gender equity and diversity while driving revenue and social impact. Through projects like Branded Content, among others, PLANO serves companies and brands such as Unilever, Seda, Bayer, Amaro, Itaú, Pepsico, DPZ&T, Heineken, Samsung, BETC, Talent, Publicis, Amaro, The Body Shop, Avon, O Boticário, Natura&Co, Sazon, and more. The consultancy also operates as an intelligence hub for ESG-related topics in partnership with Mynd, Brazil's largest influencer marketing agency.

She is the president of *Plano de Menina Institute*, a social initiative focused on empowering and connecting girls to job opportunities and scholarships through workshops on self-esteem, financial education, entrepreneurship, and career development. The institute has impacted over 5,000 girls through in-person workshops and millions more through digital content and online programs.

In August 2021, she wrote the book *Quem é você na fila do pão?* (literal translation: Who Are You in the Bread Line?), published in Brazilian Portuguese. The book is now being published in an English edition by WeBook Publishing in the Summer of 2025 in the USA and globally. *Who She Think She Is?* is a manual for turning plans into action, featuring exercises and strategies for building a successful personal brand.

Duarte is a columnist for Marie Claire magazine, a signatory of the UN Global Compact, a partner of the Consulate General of Brazil in New York, a TEDx Speaker, a Harvard Speaker, and was recognized as a Woman to Watch in 2020. She has served as a juror for the Effie Awards, was named one of Brazil's top 10 digital media professionals by M&M in 2021, and was honored as a *Paulistana Nota 10* by Veja São Paulo.

www.ingramcontent.com/pod-product-compliance
Lightning Source LLC
Chambersburg PA
CBHW031520120626
46545CB00005B/1931